"You'll never go hungry if you pack this book, which covers the state's
four major food groups: Barbecue, Steaks, Tex-Mex and Pie."
– Dallas Morning News

UPDATED

Texas Landmark Cafes

By June Naylor

Great Texas Line Press
Fort Worth, Texas

Texas Landmark Cafes

For bulk sales
and wholesale inquiries
contact:
Great Texas Line Press
Post Office Box 11105
Fort Worth, TX 76110
greattexas@hotmail.com
www.greattexasline.com
817-922-8929

*To see our complete list of Texas guide books, humor books and
cookbooks, visit greattexasline.com*

Editor: Amy Culbertson
Cover Art: George Toomer
Book design: Tom Johanningmeier

Great Texas Line Press strives to be socially responsible, donating a portion
of proceeds from several books to Habitat for Humanity of Fort Worth,
North Fort Worth Historical Society, Texas Dance Hall Preservation Inc. and
Terlingua's Big Bend Educational Foundation. Hundreds of books are donated
annually to Public Radio stations throughout Texas for fund-raising. Every
effort is made to engage Texas writers, editors, illustrators, designers and
photographers who fell victim to the newspaper industry crisis, and to
produce the books at local family-run print shops.

Introduction

In a world that keeps us overscheduled and disconnected, we long for those days when folks gathered at the downtown cafe for gossip and good food.

Each Texas town had its locals' favorite, where we went for our regular plate of biscuits and gravy, a chicken-fried steak or a bowl of chili. We had the usual afternoon catch-up over coffee and a slice of coconut meringue pie. There was a weekly stop at the barbecue pit for some smoked brisket and slow-simmered pintos, or at the drugstore soda fountain for a grilled cheese sandwich and a root-beer float, or at the Tex-Mex cafe for cheese enchiladas covered in chili gravy. (That's why we joke that the four food groups in Texas are steak, barbecue, Tex-Mex and pie.)

It's this sort of food that still helps Texans function properly; during the stretch of summer's blistering days and those bone-chilling nights when a blue norther blows in, our own special cuisine can give us the will to go on. And the camaraderie at the counter and around the tables is every bit as important.

Fortunately, the Lone Star State's roadsides are still lined with places that serve up this kind of sustenance in an uncomplicated, reassuring style that's been a trademark of Texas cuisine almost since the end of the cattle-drive era around 1886.

We treasure these vittles and the places that provide them. In a world consumed with checking e-mail, charging iPads and navigating traffic snarls, we need comfort as never before. There's something about warming up to a bowl of chicken and dumplings that's darned near as reassuring as a big, heartfelt hug.

Texas cafes with that small-town yesteryear feel are places where we can take refuge during the rough patches in life. These days, some may be thoroughly modern while still managing to evoke that small-town Texas spirit. In choosing the spots to include in this book, we looked for places that offer authenticity and are beloved by locals; places that, if not timeworn, offer a sense of nostalgia, an appreciation for true Texas food traditions. These are eateries, we find, that complete the towns or neighborhoods where they are; folks wouldn't know what to do without them.

We seek out these cafes on road trips, and we're especially relieved when we find escapes from the chain wastelands that clutter our cities and suburbs. We hunt down these places when craving something real, something crafted with care. And sometimes, these days, in cities from Houston to Austin and even in towns in the Big Bend, we're finding what we're looking for in the form of food trucks.

In this book you'll find 110 cafes across Texas, carefully chosen for offering necessary, gratifying food and for providing a sense of escaping to a simpler time when our modern world beats us down.

We think most of these cafes are worth a day trip, and you could plot entire itineraries around the cafes you'd like to try as you travel. We've organized them into seven geographic regions: Big Bend, Central Texas and the Hill Country, East Texas, Gulf Coast, North Texas, Panhandle Plains and South Texas. And, because the big cities still have venerable neighborhood spots treasured by their regulars, as well as fabled barbecue joints where the hungry may start lining up hours before the ribs are ready, we kick off the book with a chapter called City Classics.

For each cafe, we'll tell you why you want to go there, some insider info and a few top picks from the kitchen. In the "Details" section of each entry, you'll find the hours of operation and whether you can get beer, wine or cocktails, as well as a "cash only" note for restaurants that don't take credit cards.

Whether you stop for a chili dog and buttermilk pie in Pampa, chicken-fried steak and meringue pie in Strawn or a pile of smoked beef brisket and pork shoulder on butcher paper in Lockhart, you'll find each one a celebration of honest-to-goodness pure Texas chow.

— *June Naylor, Fort Worth*

Contents

8

City Classics

Avenue B Grocery
4403 Avenue B, Austin
512-453-3921, avenuebgrocery.com

Why go: Known as Austin's oldest continuously operated grocery, this charming little 1909 landmark still stocks a few staples but mostly offers deli service. Tucked away in Austin's serene old Hyde Park neighborhood, it's a place you can't help but fall in love with at first sight: Its white wooden siding, well-worn 7Up sign above the awning and Rainbo Bread screen doors are a genuine ode to the past.

In the know: Call-in orders are OK, except at high noon, when the place is just too busy. Fear not, there are picnic tables offered for your dining pleasure.

Picks: You can't go wrong with any of the sandwiches; they're made to order with good ingredients, thought and care. The King Combo sandwich includes roast beef, turkey, ham and three cheeses — but why not add avocado, banana peppers and garlic-habanero mayo to that and have them put it on dark rye? If you're needing special attention, the Queen B combines avocado, three cheeses, mushrooms and jalapeño, and you can have that on gluten-free bread. Oh, go ahead and have a deviled egg, too.

Details: Lunch Mon-Sat; closed Sun. No bar.

Cisco's Restaurant Bakery
1511 E. Sixth St., Austin
512-478-2420

Why go: An East Austin legend since 1948, this bakery and restaurant is all about home cooking. The most unpretentious place you'll find in town, it's not where you'll go if you're counting calories.

In the know: A favorite among UT fans, Cisco's offers decades of Longhorn memorabilia on the walls. If street parking is taken, look across the street for a parking lot. The only change in a long, long time is a new mural on an exterior wall.

Picks: At breakfast, try the huevos rancheros with sausage patties or the migas with a side of fajita steak or chorizo. Breakfast tacos are excellent, too. Lunch specials we love include carne guisada, beef enchiladas and crispy beef tacos.

Details: Breakfast and lunch daily. Bar.

Franklin Barbecue
900 E. 11th St., Austin
512-653-1187, franklinbbq.com

Why go: Since the moment it opened in a humble trailer in 2009, this barbecue joint has had monumentally long lines every day. The transition to brick and mortar in 2011 didn't shorten the wait times much, and ever since it was chosen as the best barbecue restaurant in the state by *Texas Monthly* in 2013, the lines just keep getting longer. Some people even pay students and other willing helpers to stand in line for them.

In the know: You can order in advance and skip the line, but the minimum order is 5 pounds of whatever you're eating. And you'll need to pick it up at opening time, 10:30 a.m.

Picks: The beef brisket is, simply, to die for. There's a dark, lush salt-and-pepper crust on the outside, flavored by post-oak smoke. The beef is all-natural, and though a sauce isn't necessary, it's hard to turn down pitmaster Aaron Franklin's espresso-based barbecue sauce. Pulled pork, sausage and pork ribs are mighty fine, too.

Details: Lunch Tue-Sun; closed Mon. Beer and wine.

Kerbey Lane Cafe
3704 Kerbey Lane, Austin
512-451-1436, kerbeylanecafe.com

Why go: Since 1980, this beloved eatery has been an homage to creatively conceived, expertly executed casual food. Fresh, all-natural ingredients never tasted so good.

In the know: Of Kerbey Lane's several locations around Austin, the original spot (on Kerbey Lane, natch) holds the most nostalgia. The menu offers lots of options for vegans and for gluten-avoiders, and there's always a page of seasonal specials (check the website and Facebook). The original Kerbey Lane used to be open 24/7 but now has cut back a bit; you can still get a bison Frito pie at 4 a.m. there on weekend nights, though (see "Details" below).

Picks: Cinnamon roll pancakes, apple pie pancakes and the Kerbey Scramble are faves for breakfast. At lunch and dinner, we love the pork belly banh mi and the Greek lamb burger, as well as the enchiladas and tacos al pastor.

Details: Open continuously from 6:30 a.m. Thu to 11 p.m. Sun.; 6:30 a.m.-11 p.m. Mon-Wed (all other locations open 24/7). Beer and wine.

Magnolia Cafe
920 S. Congress Ave., Austin
512-445-0000, themagnoliacafe.com

Why go: The groovy 1970s vibe that continues to define some aspects of Austin seems alive and well in a 21st-century kind of way at Magnolia Cafe. It's open around the clock, and the people-watching on South Congress is as good as the food (the original Magnolia Cafe is at 2304 Lake Austin Blvd.).

In the know: Be prepared to wait in line for a table at almost any hour, but know that the wait is well worth it. You may get a better chance of quick seating if you take a patio table. Vegetarians have a lot to love here.

Picks: The gingerbread pancakes are heaven, as is the breakfast plate of migas. Ancho chicken enchiladas and the spinach enchiladas get high marks, as do bison blue-cheese burgers and hummus veggie wrap (add avocado, for sure).

Details: Open 24 hours. Beer and wine.

Nau's Enfield Drug
1115 W. Lynn St., Austin
512-476-3663, nausdrug.com

Why go: Opened in 1951, this mainstay in the Clarksville neighborhood has been treasured for holding true to its origins. Seemingly nothing has changed at what's billed as the city's first full-service drugstore and soda fountain. The signage alone speaks to the days of bobby-sox and poodle skirts. The soda fountain and grill appear to be exactly as they looked generations ago, with a curved counter fronted by swiveling bar stools and additional seating at wooden booths and tables with ice cream parlor chairs.

In the know: Breakfast — some of which can be had for about five bucks — is served all day on Sunday. And true to Austin's laid-back vibe, you can get lunch until 4:15 p.m. (3:30 on Sundays).

Picks: Morning meals can be as simple as an egg with bacon and toast or a cherry Danish, or as elaborate as bacon-cheese-tomato-onion omelet with hash browns and English muffin. At lunch, favorites include the BLT sandwich and the tomato stuffed with chicken salad. For treats, there are shakes in a multitude of flavors, including pineapple and banana; sundaes; and ice cream floats (make ours a Dr Pepper float, please).

Details: Breakfast and lunch daily. No bar.

Threadgill's
6416 N. Lamar Blvd., Austin
512-451-5440, threadgills.com

Why go: Famous for its Southern-style cooking, friendly service, live music and Austin heritage, this 1930s landmark is a place you should have heard about, unless you've just arrived from another planet. It's owned today by the creators of the now-defunct Armadillo World Headquarters, and there's lot of museum to this cafe.

In the know: There's a second location at 301 W. Riverside Drive, opened in 1981. Both offer a Sunday breakfast buffet with live music from 10 a.m. until 1 p.m., as well as Howdy Hour, weekdays from 3 until 6 p.m.

Picks: The tender chicken-fried steak has earned legions of fans, as have the cornbread muffins with jalapeños and the gooey peach cobbler. A long list of vegetable side dishes includes Creole cabbage, San Antonio squash and broccoli-rice casserole.

Details: Lunch and dinner daily; breakfast/brunch Sun. Full bar.

AllGood Cafe
2934 Main St., Dallas
214-742-5362, allgoodcafe.com

Why go: Perched on a corner in Deep Ellum, this live-music venue serves up excellent down-home food. Service is friendly in the hipster vein, and the setting feels very Austin. Open just since 2000, it feels like a place you've been going to forever.

In the know: Weekend breakfast hours tend to stay very crowded, but any wait you encounter is worth your trouble. The kitchen uses ingredients from local sources (farmers' markets, Dallas Mozzarella Co., Jimmy's Food Store, Rudy's Tortillas, among others) to create food you won't likely forget. "Two-Fer Tuesdays" gets you a second entrée free.

Picks: Our breakfast favorite is the huevos rancheros with black beans, either atop a grilled steak or with peppered bacon and a short stack alongside. At lunch, it's the grilled cheddar-pepperjack sandwich with green chiles on sourdough. For dinner, we can't resist the braised short ribs or the grilled pork chop with seven-spice rub.

Details: Breakfast and lunch daily; dinner Tue-Sat. Full bar.

Highland Park Soda Fountain
3229 Knox St., Dallas
214-521-2126, highlandparksodafountain.com

Why go: Inside a former pharmacy, the 1912 landmark is still called Highland Park Pharmacy by those of us who've been visiting its lunch counter since childhood. A trolley line once connected Knox Street to the area around SMU, and some senior customers can be heard telling great-grandchildren about riding the trolley to enjoy a sarsaparilla. The pharmacy moved out in 2010, but the soda fountain and lore remain intact. Take one of 19 stools at the counter and just try not to spin around like a kid. Ice cream parlor tables offer more seating, as well.

In the know: Some folks visit the pharmacy every day for breakfast or lunch. If one of the regulars doesn't show up, the staff checks to be sure everything's OK. That's customer service.

Picks: For the morning meal, you can't wrong with eggs, biscuits and gravy, pecan waffles, English muffins or bagels. The signature items, however, are chicken salad or pimiento cheese on toast, the grilled peanut butter and jelly sandwich, Frito chili pie and sweets like a hot-fudge brownie sundae, pineapple malts and ice cream sodas.

Details: Breakfast, lunch and early dinner daily. No bar.

Lockhart Smokehouse
400 W. Davis St., Dallas
214-944-5521,lockhartsmokehouse.com

Why go: Just as the Bishop Arts District was becoming hyper-hot for all its fine-cuisine restaurants, here came a barbecue joint true to its Central Texas heritage. The owners descend from the Kreuz Market family in Lockhart and offer an authentic taste of oak-smoked meats from that glorious part of the state.

In the know: While originally offering their food on butcher paper with no sauce or forks — as is the style in the old-fashioned places — Lockhart's owners realized that city folks couldn't accept such traditions easily. Sauce and forks are now offered, but they aren't needed.

Picks: Brisket with a dark, thick crust is outstanding. Beef shoulder clod is leaner and exceptionally good. Pork chops can't be beaten, and the jalapeño-cheese sausage will become your favorite. Don't pass up the deviled eggs.

Details: Lunch and dinner daily. Full bar. Second location in Plano.

Mama's Daughters' Diner

2014 Irving Blvd., Dallas
214-742-8646, mamasdaughtersdiner.com

Why go: Open for more than 50 years near the Design District, the medical centers and the market halls, this folksy cafe makes you feel at home the moment you walk in the door. Far from fancy, it's simply a place to be treated well while eating good food.

In the know: Several other locations are scattered around the area.

Picks: At breakfast, the spinach-cheese omelet is a good bet, as are pecan waffles and fried-egg sandwiches. For lunch, daily specials range from baked chicken, meatloaf and liver and onions on Monday to chicken and dumplings on Wednesday and salmon patties and breaded catfish on Friday. Chicken-fried steak and fried chicken are offered daily.

Details: Breakfast, lunch and dinner Mon-Fri; breakfast and lunch Sat; closed Sun. No bar.

Norma's Cafe

1123 W. Davis St., Dallas
214-946-2111, normascafe.com

Why go: Opened in the 1950s, this Oak Cliff gem has stayed the same while the neighborhood around it fell and rose again. The food, particularly the Mile-High Cream Pies, feels like time has stood still. And yet Norma's keeps an active Facebook page.

In the know: Norma's has a big heart, hosting a free Thanksgiving dinner every year on Thanksgiving to anyone in need and offering a number of fund-raisers for local charities from its original location as well as at its stores in North Dallas and Frisco.

Picks: The Mexican breakfast dishes are as good as the French toast and Belgian waffles. At lunch and dinner, good choices include smothered steak, fried chicken, beef tips with noodles, smoked brisket, burgers and meatloaf.

Details: Breakfast, lunch and dinner daily. No bar.

Pecan Lodge
2702 Main St., Dallas
214-748-8900, pecanlodge.com

Why go: In its original small stand in the Dallas Farmers Market, Pecan Lodge developed such a devoted following for its killer barbecue that it had to move to this new site after just three years. Customers standing in long, long lines now have more space in which to enjoy the remarkable eats.

In the know: The owners were hugely successful in the management consulting business before giving themselves over fully to their barbecue passion. Their mobile barbecue pit, named Lurlene, gives them catering abilities, too.

Picks: Smoked beef brisket is luscious, as are the fried chicken and the shrimp and grits.

Details: Lunch Tue-Thu and Sun, dinner Fri-Sat; closed Mon. BYOB.

Sonny Bryan's Smokehouse
2202 Inwood Road, Dallas
214-357-7120, sonnybryans.com

Why go: Since 1910, Sonny Bryan's has been known throughout Texas and the South as a place for good old-fashioned barbecue. Though Sonny's has grown to include several locations, the original on Inwood remains the favorite among its loyal clientele.

In the know: The tiny original store recently expanded to include additional seating. While it's not the same as eating barbecue on the hood of your car, it's nice to be able to sit inside when the elements aren't favorable. We still prefer to eat our barbecue at the itty-bitty school desks in the older part of the building.

Picks: Brisket, ribs and sausage are the mainstays, but the pulled chicken and pulled pork shouldn't be overlooked. French fries are excellent, as are the onion rings.

Details: Lunch and dinner daily. Beer.

Sweet Georgia Brown

2840 E. Ledbetter Drive, Dallas
214-375-2020

Why go: This longtime favorite in South Dallas has been the city's go-to spot for soul food, and it's gained even more fans since the beloved Vern's closed down. You don't go for décor or fancy settings; rather, it's the enormous servings of stick-to-your-ribs goodness — served on disposable plates — that bring you back, time and again.

In the know: Found south of downtown Dallas on Loop 12 between I-45 and I-35, this is a good stop for lunch before a visit and long walk around the nearby Dallas Zoo. And keep in mind that lunch is a better option, as the kitchen may run out of some favorites by the evening meal.

Picks: In addition to the barbecue — notably sliced brisket and sausage — we like the fried chicken and fried pork chops. Everybody raves about the sides — rice and gravy, succotash, sweet potatoes, mac and cheese, broccoli rice, cucumber salad. Almost nobody ever has room for dessert, but those who do usually order peach cobbler.

Details: Lunch and dinner daily. No bar.

Avila's Mexican Food
6232 N. Mesa, El Paso
915-584-3621, avilas.com

Why go: A 1952 institution, this beloved fixture in the community is decorated with fancy Mexican tilework and wooden santos. Award-winning and beloved by critics from coast to coast, Avila's has the distinction of cooking at the folklife festival hosted by the Smithsonian in Washington, D.C.

In the know: Dessert is the traditional sopaipillas — fluffy, hot pillows dusted with cinnamon and sugar. Drizzling honey on top is gilding the lily, but just do it anyway.

Picks: Start with the aged, white-cheese queso studded with Hatch chiles and panko-crusted, fried avocado slices. The soup of choice is the slow-cooked beef with potatoes and chiles, served with tortillas. Among tacos, the top choice is picadillo, a fried-to-order hard-shell corn tortilla holding spicy ground beef flecked with potatoes and minced chiles, along with white cheddar cheese shreds, lettuce and tomato.

Details: Lunch and dinner, Mon-Sat, lunch only Sun. Credit cards. Full bar.

Good Luck Cafe
3813 Alameda Ave., El Paso
915-532-9039, goodluckcafe.net

Why go: Opened as the Good Luck Tavern downtown in the 1960s, the Good Luck moved to its current place in 1988. Always run by the same family, it's hugely popular with the local community. Super-friendly staff and good food keep generations of fans happy.

In the know: Near one of the international bridges to Juarez, the

Good Luck blends Mexican cafe and American home cooking.

Picks: Morning dishes include huevos a la Mexicana, hot-cakes and menudo. At lunch and dinner, burgers, chile con carne, chiles rellenos and T-bone steak will fill you up. For dessert, check out the tres leches cake or empanadas.

Details: Breakfast, lunch and dinner Thu-Tue; closed Wed. No bar.

H&H Car Wash
701 E. Yandell Drive, El Paso
915-533-1144

Why go: Since 1958, this diamond in the rough has been a favorite among foodies who love insider places. It's been covered by *Food & Wine* magazine. Julia Child tried it (and loved it) when she visited El Paso. It's been awarded a James Beard honor for regional cuisine, for Pete's sake. For handmade, down-home Mexican food, you can't do better than this little lunch counter inside a car wash, where you can get your car hand-cleaned for a song, too.

In the know: It's incredibly modest, tiny and unlikely looking. Service can be brusque. Because it seats only a small crowd at once, you want to go at an off hour or be prepared to wait. Breakfast is served at any time, too.

Picks: Huevos rancheros and steak-and-egg tacos rank high in our book. At lunch, get the chile relleno.

Details: Breakfast and lunch Mon-Sat; closed Sun. No bar.

L&J Cafe
3622 E. Missouri Ave., El Paso
915-566-8418, landjcafe.com

Why go: This El Paso landmark opened as Tony's Place in 1927 and operated as a bootleggers' joint, frequented regularly by soldiers from nearby Fort Bliss. The name change came in 1968, and it's remained a beloved no-frills spot ever since. The signage and both exterior and interior tell you it's a dive, it's a bar — but a plate of food tells you that the kitchen knows its way around Mexican comfort specialties.

In the know: The restaurant tagline reads "The old place by the graveyard" for good reason. The cafe sits immediately west of historic Concordia Cemetery.

Picks: Solace is found in bowls of hot chicken or beef soup, filled with vegetables and served with tortillas and rice on the side. A West Texas specialty, the tampiqueña plate is a sirloin or T-bone steak (or chicken, if you must), topped with grilled green-chile strips and a cheese enchilada in red chile sauce, with rice, beans and guacamole on the side. Desebrada tacos are filled with shredded beef. Watch for specials such as chicken in mole sauce and gorditas. For breakfast, try the huevos divorciados, two eggs topped with both red and green chile sauces.

Details: Breakfast, lunch and dinner daily. Beer and wine.

Lucy's Cafe
1305 N. Mesa St., El Paso
915-534-7421

Why go: Since 1972, when its owner struck out on her own from H&H Car Wash, this friendly coffee shop with a loyal following has offered seating at a counter close to the griddle, where you can watch the machaca and the eggs sizzle.

In the know: There's a second Lucy's at 4119 N. Mesa, and a third location opened in late 2013 at 6600 N. Mesa.

Picks: Huevos rancheros is a good bet for breakfast: Served atop a corn tortilla, the eggs get a decoration of onion, tomato and green chile, with crispy hash browns alongside. The machaca burrito, blending the best of old Mexico and Tex-Mex with shredded beef, onion, chiles and queso, is a big hit, too, as is the legendary machaca plate.

Details: Breakfast, lunch and early dinner Mon-Fri; breakfast and lunch Sat; closed Sun. No bar.

Drew's Place
5701 Curzon Ave., Fort Worth
817-735-4408, drewssoulfood.com

Why go: We make a beeline for this soul-food haven on the edge of Fort Worth's Ridglea neighborhood when the hankering for hand-made fried chicken sets in. Family-run and as friendly as anyplace in town, Drew's often has a line out the door at high noon. There's adequate seating inside, but lots of folks who can't wait to eat take their orders to go if the restaurant is too crowded.

In the know: That fried chicken is made to order, so either call ahead or be prepared to wait 20 minutes or so. You can tide yourself over with corn muffins. If you're eating light, try the LeeAnn Plate, offering smaller portions.

Picks: In addition to fried chicken, there's smothered pork chops, fried catfish and a legion of sides, like collard greens, fried okra, red beans, mac and cheese, black-eyed peas, fried corn on the cob and candied yams. For dessert: pecan pie and sweet-potato pie.

Details: Lunch and early dinner Tue-Sat; closed Sun-Mon. No bar.

Esperanza's Mexican Bakery & Cafe
2122 N. Main St., Fort Worth
817-626-5770, joets.com

Why go: A popular little sister to the legendary Joe T. Garcia's, this Mexican Cafe opened by Joe T.'s daughter, Hope, just keeps growing more famous in its own right. A source of solid Tex-Mex food, it's also a destination for dishes from Mexico's interior.

In the know: Crowds can be huge at breakfast and lunch peak hours, so plan accordingly. If the weather is nice, ask for a patio table. There's a second location, too, that keeps later hours, at 1601 Park Place Ave., off Eighth Avenue on the Near South Side.

Picks: Papas con huevos (potatoes and eggs) and huevos a la Mexicana with chorizo and cheese are exceptional at breakfast, as are the pancakes. At lunch, the soups are outstanding, along with the ceviche tostada, enchiladas, carne guisada and shrimp dishes. From the bakery, grab some empanadas on the way out.

Details: Breakfast, lunch and early dinner daily. Cash only. Full bar.

Old Neighborhood Grill
1633 Park Place Ave., Fort Worth
817-923-2282

Why go: A gathering spot for the Near South Side, Mistletoe Heights, Berkeley and TCU crowds, this simple but solid, homey, uber-friendly cafe does fresh food well. It's not fancy, but it's not a dive, either, and it offers something for everyone. In fact, it's the exemplar of a neighborhood restaurant.

In the know: Although it's known for chicken-fried steak and pot roast, there are lighter options worth consideration, as well as some more contemporary specials like the occasional quail kabobs. You can assemble your ideal veggie plate from the long roster of side dishes offered, including puckery pickled green tomatoes, moist corn fritters and superior greens.

Picks: Meatloaf and fried chicken are favorites, as are the burgers. Leaner choices are salmon with fresh veggies and a variety of salads. Of course, there are the desserts, which can sabotage any virtuous visitor.

Details: Breakfast, lunch and dinner Mon-Sat; closed Sun. Beer and wine.

Paris Coffee Shop
704 W. Magnolia Ave., Fort Worth
817-335-4021, pariscoffeeshop.net

Why go: Opened in the late 1920s, the Paris is run today by Mike Smith, the son of its founder, and it's still a favorite of Fort Worth's old guard. Most of the customers have been regulars for years, and Mike makes sure they are treated to warm hospitality.

In the know: Thursday lunch features chicken and dumplings, so look for bigger crowds that day. At the noon hour, the line for tables can be long, so bring a pocketful of patience with you.

Picks: The Greek omelet is our breakfast favorite, closely followed by fried eggs with corned beef hash. There's also a cinnamon roll of obscene size. At lunch, chicken-fried steak, grilled pork chops and chicken and dumplings are all big draws. Mike's proud of his pies; among the most popular are coconut, lemon, chocolate meringue and egg custard.

Details: Breakfast and lunch Mon-Fri; breakfast only Sat; closed Sun. No bar.

West Side Cafe
7050 Camp Bowie West, Fort Worth
817-560-1996

Why go: "Country cookin" reads the sign (don't worry, the "tattoo" mentioned below is for a neighboring establishment), and West Side lives up to that promise. A longtime favorite in the far west end of Fort Worth, this place doesn't look like much from the outside, but the legions of cars in the parking lot will give you a clue as to its popularity. Inside, it's big and warm and bustling with the energy of folks who come here at least once or twice a week and a staff that knows all the regulars — and there are many — by name. Even if they don't know your name, they'll make you feel glad you showed up.

In the know: Locals come to this western reach of town to buy cars at the dealerships just a bit farther west along the boulevard and to shop at Fiesta, a grocery chain based in Houston. Like your bacon extra-crisp or your eggs extra-soft? Ask and ye shall receive. This is one of those extremely rare places where you can order your food cooked exactly the way you like it and get it cooked exactly that way, every time. And breakfast, praise the lord, is served all day.

Picks: Mornings are happier with a plate of pancakes or a Western omelet in front of you. At the noon hour or for supper, try the exemplary chicken-fried steak, with real mashed potatoes or squash casserole on the side. You'll find some of the city's better pies here, along with homey banana pudding.

Details: Breakfast, lunch and dinner daily. No bar.

The Breakfast Klub
3711 Travis St., Houston
713-528-8561, thebreakfastklub.com

Why go: The line around the block, found just about any hour TBK is open, should tell you this is a place with food to be savored. It's a landmark in Houston's Midtown, with a friendly owner in Marcus Davis.

In the know: Local politicians consider this a prime meeting spot at breakfast and lunch. Many a deal has been brokered here over plates of hearty food.

Picks: Grilled buttermilk biscuits with sausage pan gravy, fried eggs and pork chops with grits, crispy wings with waffles and catfish with crawfish étouffée are among standouts.

Details: Breakfast and lunch daily. No bar.

Gatlin's BBQ
1221 W. 19th St., Houston
713-869-4227, gatlinsbbq.com

Why go: Open just since 2010, this family operation quickly rose to the top of its class, nabbing high honors in *Texas Monthly*'s list of top 50 barbecue joints in 2013. Housed in a little cottage in the Heights neighborhood, about four miles north of downtown, it's a homegrown treasure serving fine Texas barbecue with hints of Louisiana.

In the know: Gatlin's low-and-slow smoking is so well-loved that there's almost always a line out the door. There's not much seating inside, and only a small patio, so you might need to eat lunch on the hood of your car.

Picks: You want a plate piled with sliced brisket, pork ribs, sausage and baby back ribs. Get the chipotle sauce and sides of dirty rice, green beans, coleslaw and ranch beans. And then there's bread pudding and lemon butter pound cake for dessert.

Details: Lunch and early dinner Tue-Sat; closed Sun-Mon. No bar.

Irma's Restaurant
22 N. Chenevert St., Houston
713-222-0767, irmasoriginal.com

Why go: Occupying an older brick building near Minute Maid Park in downtown Houston, this place may not look too special from the outside. But inside, the convivial spirit makes you think you've stepped into the breakfast room of someone's home. Everyone seems to know each other, and the staff treats you like you've always been around — even it's your first visit.

In the know: Something new is on the menu every day; Irma keeps everyone guessing, but it's always a home-style Mexican dish. Irma's may be pricier than some; that may be the price you pay for a place that's been featured on the Food Network. In pretty weather, patio seating is the way to go.

Picks: There's no menu, per se. The staff tells you what's offered, and it's usually enchiladas, tamales, tacos, burritos and fajitas. The shrimp tacos are outstanding. The lemonade is a fruity, bright eye-opener that shouldn't be missed.

Details: Breakfast and lunch Mon-Fri; dinner Thu-Sat; closed Sun. If the Astros are playing at home during the week, Irma's is open until 7 p.m. Full bar.

Spanish Village

4720 Almeda, Houston
713-523-2861, spanishvillagerestaurant.com

Why go: An institution for more than half a century — Larry Mc-Murtry gave it an uncredited cameo in his 1970 novel *Moving On* — this sprawling Tex-Mex landmark feels pleasantly stuck in time. While it may have gone a little rough at the edges, it's the place to go when you want to escape all signs of the modern world.

In the know: The quirky enclosed dining porch, garlanded with strands of festive Christmas lights, is the sentimental favorite spot for the quintessential Spanish Village experience. Longtime patrons swear by the fried chicken — no kidding!

Picks: Fresh lime margaritas, partially frozen and served in an old-fashioned martini glass, are some of the best authentic, unadulterated version you can find. The cheese enchiladas are legitimately iconic. Combo plates are popular; No. 26 gives you a cheese-and-onion enchilada, beef taco and a chalupa — that's a toasted tortilla topped with beans, cheese, guacamole, lettuce and tomato.

Details: Lunch and dinner Tue-Sat; closed Sun-Mon. Full bar.

Virgie's Bar-B-Q

5535 N. Gessner Drive, Houston
713-466-6525, virgiesbbq.com

Why go: Opened in 2005, Virgie's is a modest but mighty pit barbecue joint that's drawn high praise from 'cue critics everywhere. Owner Adrian Handsborough, whose parents ran Virgie's first as a burger joint and then as a grocery, says his "barbecure" will cure what ails you.

In the know: Near U.S. 290 in the northwest part of Houston, Virgie's is worth the drive from whatever part of town in which you find yourself. Plan on early or late lunch arrival to avoid lines; if you're looking for supper, you'll have to make it an early one.

Picks: The most popular is a three-meat plate, loaded with oak-smoked beef brisket, pork ribs and beef link sausage. Ask for potato salad, baked beans and coleslaw on the side. An alternative is the baked potato stuffed with chopped beef barbecue.

Details: Lunch Tue-Sat; early dinner Wed-Sat; closed Sun. No bar.

Chris Madrids
1900 Blanco Rd., San Antonio
210-735-3552, chrismadrids.com

Why go: Simple but always satisfying, this burger joint is a sprawling site (two adjoining buildings) with a huge patio and a relatively small menu. Open for 40 years in an older neighborhood (Beacon Hill, near Montevista) not far from downtown, this place has grown into a legend.

In the know: Go for late lunch or early dinner to avoid the longer wait in line to order. The line moves pretty fast, all things considered, but you'll want someone to save you a table while you join the queue to order.

Picks: The Cheddar Cheezy is the big favorite, a burger either one-quarter or half-pound in size, topped with melted cheddar, mustard, lettuce, pickles and tomato. The Tostada Burger is hard to pass up, with a topping of refried beans, chips, onion, melted cheddar and salsa. Just don't even think about skipping the hand-cut fries.

Details: Lunch and dinner, Mon-Sat. Credit cards. Full bar.

Earl Abel's Restaurant
1201 Austin Highway, San Antonio
210-822-3358, earlabelssa.com

Why go: Among the oldest eating establishments in SAT, this old-fashioned favorite opened in 1933. There's comfort in sitting down to dinner in a place our grandparents may have loved. Most customers return time and again for the pies, but the fried chicken is legendary as well.

In the know: New owners took over in 2007, keeping the traditional items but adding more contemporary offerings. Now there's a roster of salads to balance out the heavier fried options.

Picks: For breakfast, there's venison sausage from Texas' Broken Arrow Ranch, served with two eggs. At lunch and dinner, the bison burger is a modern option, while the fried chicken and chicken-fried steak are good go-tos. Among pies, there's meringue with chocolate, lemon or coconut filling, as well as apple, cherry and pecan. Other sweets to note include éclairs, layer cakes and sweet rolls.

Details: Breakfast, lunch and dinner daily. Beer and wine.

El Mirador
722 S. St. Mary's St., San Antonio
210-225-9444, elmiradorrestaurant.com

Why go: This venerable and popular gathering place has a loyal local following (including plenty of politicos); it's the kind of place where friends have been meeting at lunch on the same day of the week for decades. El Mirador's authenticity has always been reassuring in a world of homogenized Tex-Mex; you could find the real thing here, made the same way for generations. Changes may be coming, though; the Treviño family, which opened the restaurant in 1968, sold El Mirador in 2014; it's now in the hands of a local architect and developer.

In the know: In Southtown, El Mirador is the perfect place to eat before or after a King William District driving or walking tour to see the impressive architecture favored by San Antonio's mostly German gentry in the 1800s.

Picks: At breakfast, the chilaquiles (tortilla strips with scrambled eggs, pico de gallo and ranchero sauce) and huevos rancheros are big favorites. At lunch, the daily soups are legendary, especially Saturday's sopa Azteca.

Details: Breakfast and lunch daily; dinner Mon-Sat. Full bar.

Mi Tierra Cafe y Panaderia
218 Produce Row in Market Square (El Mercado)
San Antonio
210-225-1262, mitierracafe.com

Why go: Open since 1941 in the largest Mexican market north of the Rio Grande, Mi Tierra is not only an institution but a pioneer of Tex-Mex cuisine. Open 24 hours a day and decorated with Christmas lights all year long, it's famous for strolling mariachis, strong margaritas and cold beer. Wander the rooms to marvel at murals, tile work, vintage photography and happy people eating hearty food.

In the know: At peak hours, this restaurant is extremely crowded — even though it seats 500 people. Go at off times or sip a margarita in the bar while you wait for a table. And don't leave without some of the tempting sweets from the bakery cases.

Picks: Breakfast, always available, is great; any of the egg dishes will please. Lunch and dinner standouts include tortilla soup, green-chile enchiladas, steak tampiqueña and chicken flautas.

Details: Always open. Full bar.

Two Bros. BBQ Market
12656 West Ave., San Antonio
210-496-0222, twobrosbbqmarket.com

Why go: There really are two brothers behind this contemporary barbecue joint, a downscale effort from two upscale chefs. Jason and Jake Dady, whose restaurant work has traditionally been of the white-tablecloth variety, stretched new muscles when opening Two Bros. in 2008. Named to *Texas Monthly*'s top-50 barbecue list in 2013, Two Bros. found itself featured in (and on the cover of) *Texas Monthly* barbecue editor Daniel Vaughn's book *The Prophets of Smoked Meat* that same year.

In the know: Even jalapeños and shrimp get the smoke treatment here, the former stuffed with cream cheese and wrapped in bacon, the latter chilled; both are addictive appetizers. Be warned that the more popular goods sell out early.

Picks: Family-style is the way to go. The "2 Bros." combo provides a half-pound of brisket, half-pound of smoked pork butt and half-pound of pork ribs, plus sausage, two chicken thighs and a choice of two sides. Don't dare skip the fried strawberry pies.

Details: Lunch and early dinner daily. Beer.

Big Bend

Basin Burger House

607 N. Colorado St., Midland
432-687-5696, basinburgerhouse.com

Why go: A gourmet burger in downtown Midland? Yep, complete with European-style breads and freshly cut-to-order potatoes for fries. Inspired menu options include a brisket philly sandwich, brisket nachos and bourbon meatloaf. Breakfast is a big bonus in this friendly joint.

In the know: Sunday drink specials include bloody mary, mimosa, tequila sunrise and spiked lemonade. Watch for happy hour specials and live entertainment throughout the week.

Picks: The green chile burger scored high points in *Texas Monthly*'s roundup of the state's best burgers. The enormous patty is made with brisket, short rib and chuck and piled with avocado, jack cheese, charred poblano, grilled onions and a fried egg, and there's a roasted jalapeno aioli on the bun, too. The pork belly salad is an indulgence, and the cauliflower steak keeps vegetarians satisfied.

Details: Breakfast, Mon-Fri; lunch and dinner, Mon-Sat; breakfast and lunch, Sun. Credit cards. Full bar.

Cueva de Leon
611 Texas 118, Fort Davis
432-426-3801

Why go: Open since 1975, this favorite Mexican cafe provides plenty of fuel for hiking in the Davis Mountains State Park and for long evenings of star-gazing at nearby McDonald Observatory. Regular visitors to the area have been known to drive an extra hundred miles just to eat at this casual spot.

In the know: The Indian Lodge in the nearby state park has wonderfully comfortable rooms in its CCC-constructed building. The Limpia Hotel right in historic downtown is excellent, too. Do plan a visit to the restored cavalry fort at Fort Davis National Historic Site.

Picks: The chiles rellenos are famous throughout the region; we're also fond also of the green and red enchiladas.

Details: Lunch and dinner Mon-Sat; lunch only Sun. BYOB

La Cueva de Oso
205 N. El Paso St., Balmorhea
432-375-2273

Why go: Open since 1990, this cafe sits in the town best known for the San Solomon Springs at Balmorhea State Park. Most every visitor to this desert oasis comes to Cueva de Oso, or Cave of the Bear, for some of the most sought-after Mexican food in West Texas.

In the know: Not an especially large place, it can be plenty crowded on weekends when the park is busy. It's probably wisest to come at off-hours on the weekend to avoid a wait. Lodging tip: If you can't find a room at the park, try the newish El Oso Flojo Lodge next door.

Picks: Stacked green enchiladas, tacos and fajitas.

Details: Lunch and dinner Thu-Tue; closed Wed. Beer.

Fat Lyle's
719 S. Highland Ave., Marfa
432-295-2377

Why go: While food trucks aren't unusual by any stretch of the imagination today, this one is special and should be sought out. It sits on a lot across the highway from El Cosmico, and everyone in town knows how to find it – so just ask if you're needing help.

In the know: Place your order at the window and find a picnic table seat to call your own. If you're running short on time, call in your order before you arrive; check Fat Lyle's Facebook page to see what's cooking.

Picks: Taco Tuesday is popular, and so is any day the burgers are on the menu (try the Korean or vegan black bean). Fried chicken is a great Sunday bet, and so are random finds like beef stew and pulled pork on a bun.

Details: Lunch Fri-Tue; closed Wed-Thu. Cash only. BYOB.

Food Shark
909 W. San Antonio St., Marfa
432-207-2090, foodsharkmarfa.com

Why go: Worldwide publicity has come to this humble food truck; the chef, Krista Bork, has worked in Europe, and the front-of-the-house man, husband Adam Bork, is an artist and musician of some renown. And the food is really good, to boot.

In the know: Recently relocated on Highway 90 (San Antonio St.) to a site owner-artist-musician-chef Adam Bork calls New Foodsharkland. There, he's offering Friday evening dinners with changing menu; and "happier hour," serving beer, cider and wine.

Picks: Marfalafel, a falafel dish topped with red-chile sauce, is the signature dish. Sandwiches are always excellent. Tacos are worth the long waits in line, too — and don't pass up the cookies!

Details: Lunch Wed-Sat; dinner Friday; closed Sun-Tue. Cash only. BYOB.

Fort Davis Drug Store
113 N. State St., Fort Davis
432-426-3118, fortdavisdrugstore.net

Why go: Originally opened in the Limpia Hotel, across the street, in 1913, this quaintsy-cute soda fountain is found downstairs from the Old Texas Inn (aka the Fort Davis Hotel), a six-room hotel on the main drag of town. A friendly gathering spot for locals and folks making their way to and from Big Bend National Park, it's a great place to glean suggestions for things to see in the immediate area.

In the know: About 25 minutes south is Marfa and 20 miles east is Alpine, but you'll find plenty of interesting little shops to poke around in within a few blocks of here. Check out the art gallery at the drugstore, too, if you're a fan of Western art.

Picks: Breakfast offers eggs, bacon and pancakes, as well as biscuits and gravy and French toast. At lunch, cheeseburgers are big favorites, and there's a good club sandwich and a good chicken salad. The dinner-menu stars are rib-eye and chicken-fried steak. Soda-fountain specialties include banana splits and old-fashioned malts, made with Bluebell ice cream.

Details: Three meals daily. No bar.

Los Jalapeños Cafe
102 W. Murphy St., Alpine
432-837-5101, losjalapenoscafe.com

Why go: Chef Vidal Garcia opened Los Jalapeños in 2011 to bring his food to Texas from Chihuahua, Mexico, and Texas is better for it. Pure and comforting, the dishes speak far more of the mountains of Mexico than of the Tex-Mex we typically see.

In the know: Find the cafe just over the railroad tracks, on the far side of the Amtrak station from U.S. 90/Holland Avenue, the town's main drag. Local artwork — all for sale — hangs on the walls of the colorful Cafe. When the weather's cooperative, there's a delightful patio to the side of the cafe.

Picks: At breakfast, we're all over the huevos rancheros with red-chile sauce, as well as the huevos a la Mexicana with a side of sausage. In the evening, we like chef Vidal's specials, which may include pork loin glazed with chipotle-orange sauce, grilled quail or chicken-fried steak with jalapeño sauce. The posole is hard to beat, too.

Details: Breakfast, lunch and dinner Tue-Sun; closed Mon. BYOB.

Judy's Bread & Breakfast
113 W. Holland Ave., Alpine
432-837-9424, facebook.com/judysbreadandbreakfast

Why go: Judith Anderson's storefront cafe on Alpine's main drag is as warm and friendly as it is delicious. Inside the red-framed glass doors, we like taking a seat at one of the windows so we can be bathed in sun while we eat.

In the know: Baked goods are always available here. Try the cinnamon rolls or muffins, and plan on taking plenty to go.

Picks: The cowboy breakfast includes two eggs, a biscuit and gravy, grits or potatoes, plus bacon or sausage. The breakfast burrito is a monster; you can get all kinds of meats, cheese and veggies inside. For lunch, the corned beef and Swiss is excellent. There are plenty of vegetarian offerings, as well.

Details: Breakfast daily; lunch Mon and Wed-Sat. BYOB.

Marfa Burrito
517 S. Highland Ave., Marfa
325-514-8675

Why go: A tiny shop in the front of a private home, this place serves a killer burrito. If you're in search of ambience, you should know that this is a humble place – some would rightfully call it a dive – so go with appropriate expectations.

In the know: Speaking Spanish helps but isn't required. The proprietress, known universally as Ramona the Burrito Lady, is a most willing host. There's no menu; just ask for a burrito filled with the goodies you like and she'll do her best to accommodate.

Picks: The breakfast variety is our favorite, stuffed with eggs, cheese, potatoes and bacon. Get extra salsa and be full till supper.

Details: Early morning through early afternoon most days. Cash only. No bar.

Martinez Bakery
206 E. Florida Ave., Midland
432-683-3100

Why go: It's hard to beat any old-school Mexican bakery with an on-site café, as you know this is home-cooking at its best.

In the know: Serve yourself bottled cold drinks from the ice box and grab a platter to load with the pastries — pumpkin empanadas are tops, but the cookies and sweet rolls are deliciously fresh — and proceed to the counter. There, place your food order.

Picks: Tortas are the favorite, thanks to the plump, sweetish buns. Fill it with chicken, ham, barbacoa or fried chicken, and take on all the toppings, ie, cheese, avocado and sour cream. The order of four tacos (in homemade tortillas), dressed with chopped babae, tomato, avocado and cilantro, is hard to pass up, howver.

Details: Breakfast, lunch, dinner Tue-Sun. Credit cards. No bar.

Twister Tacos
3601 Andrews Highway, Odessa
432-363-1701

Why go: Housed in a former Taco Bell, this neighborhood go-to offers a far better menu than its fast-food predecessor. Yes, it's divey — but well worth investigating.

In the know: Despite the name, it's not all tacos here. Enchiladas are every bit as popular — and good. Burritos and quesadillas round out the selections.

Picks: Get the platter of four tacos featuring grilled steak in fresh flour tortillas with a melted cheese-stuffed roasted green chile. Another excellent choice is the trio of enchiladas, either the beef in red chile sauce or chicken in green chile, with rice and whole beans alongside. An orange Fanta is the perfect soda to go with, unless you opt for fresh limonada.

Details: Breakfast, lunch, dinner Mon-Sat. Cash only. No bar.

Central Texas & the Hill Country

Alamo Springs Café

107 Alamo Rd., Fredericksburg
830-990-8004

Why go: Sitting outside of the heart of town about 15 minutes, this destination restaurant draws visitors from San Antonio, Kerrville, Boerne and Austin, too. You reach the old dive along a winding country road near a state park with a popular bat roost in an old railroad tunnel.

In the know: Live music is often on tap, which packs the place even more than usual. Keep in mind, the restaurant is often crowded, so be prepared for a wait at peak dining times.

Picks: Towering burgers are the reason people make long treks here, and the jalapeno cheese bun is the smart choice. Peppery onion rings are a thing of beauty, too. Special other items include fried avocado and Friday night steak dinner.

Details: Lunch and dinner, Thu-Tue. Credit cards. Beer and wine.

Blue Bonnet Café
211 U.S. 281, Marble Falls
830-693-2344, bluebonnetcafe.net

Why go: A favorite among home-cooking places around the state, this one sits on well-traveled, scenic Highway 281. Even at 10:30 a.m., when most restaurants experience a midmorning lull, the Blue Bonnet may well have a line streaming out the door as patrons wait for tables.

In the know: It's widely assumed that the Blue Bonnet, being in the midst of prime bluebonnet territory, is named for the state flower, but the truth is that it was named for a lady's hat. Be aware, nonetheless, that traffic is even heavier than usual during springtime wildflower-viewing weekends. Grab a stool at the counter if you don't need a table. If you stop in between 3 and 5 p.m. on weekdays, it's pie happy hour.

Picks: For breakfast, which is served all day, try the vegetable omelet with hash browns and biscuits on the side. Popular dinners include the chicken-fried steak and fried chicken liver, as well as grilled hamburger steak with onions. Tuesday's lunch special is chicken and dumplings; Wednesday's is meatloaf. But what brings the Blue Bonnet the most notice is pie: Peanut butter, coconut meringue and fudge are among the big hits.

Details: Breakfast and lunch daily; dinner Mon-Sat. No bar.

Burton Cafe
12513 Washington St., Burton
979-289-2200, burtoncafe.com

Why go: An old cotton-gin town near Round Top, Burton is a day trip from Austin or Houston. The cafe has been open since 1936, with German and American specialties standing the test of time.

In the know: Live music is offered Friday evenings. And during Oktoberfest, there's everything from a ceremonial keg-tapping to wiener-dog races, barrel races and a big chicken dance.

Picks: At breakfast, have eggs and German pancakes with bacon or sausage. At dinner, choices include rib-eye or veal schnitzel with pan fries and salad, sauerbraten or rouladen with red cabbage and German fries, grilled chicken with cheese spaetzle. There are bratwurst and burgers, too. Pastries are delightful.

Details: Breakfast, lunch and dinner Thu-Sat; breakfast and lunch only Sun; closed Mon-Wed. Beer and wine.

Cassandra's Soulfood & Seafood
874 S. Fort Hood St., Killeen
254-213-3661, cassandrasseafood.com

Why go: Louisiana flavors are on tap at Cassandra's, a place close to the sprawling and busy Fort Hood Army base. If you're really in search of a Mardi Gras mood, Friday night brings live music.

In the know: Portions are huge, so order accordingly.

Picks: Starters include crawfish cornbread, fried crawfish, frog legs and alligator bites. Oyster, shrimp or crawfish po'boy sandwiches and crawfish étouffée over rice bring you a taste of Cajun country. Daily specials (served from 10:30 a.m. to 3 p.m.) include smothered pork chops, oxtails and fried-to-order chicken, along with sides like okra and tomatoes.

Details: Lunch and dinner daily. Full bar.

Cooper's Old Time Pit Bar-B-Que

604 W. Young St., Llano
325-247-5713, coopersbbqllano.com

Why go: Open since 1962, this legendary favorite has an asset that sets it apart from most others, and that's its rustic but impressive presentation: You can see all the smoked meats offered in one breathtaking broad look. As you approach the front door of this sprawling no-frills barbecue emporium, you'll encounter a smoky compound of long metal pits being tended by the pitmaster. He'll lift up the heavy cover, allowing you a view of a panoply of burnished meats lined up on the grill — brisket, sausage, beef and pork ribs, sirloin and T-bone steaks, pork chops and pork loin, half and whole chickens, prime rib. You get to pick out what you want, and you *will* end up choosing too much.

In the know: After you've made your selections from the pit, you take your tray loaded with meats inside to be weighed and paid for; that's where you can add potato salad and coleslaw to your order. Find a seat at the community-style long tables, then grab some iced tea and ladle yourself out some good complementary pintos from tables at the far end of the dining room. Llano is especially busy in the fall hunting season, so don't be surprised to find a huge crowd on weekends leading up to the holidays; fine spring weekends in wildflower season are equally frantic. And come early if you want to nab some cabrito or chicken; they sell out quickly.

Picks: Smoked sirloin steak is a prize, as are rib-eyes (Thu-Sat dinner only), monster pork chops, brisket, goat, chicken and beef ribs. Blackberry cobbler tops the cobbler roster.

Details: Lunch and dinner daily. Beer. (Find a Cooper's also in Fort Worth.)

Cypress Creek Inn
408 Texas 27, Comfort
830-995-3977, cypresscreekinn.com

Why go: The longtime favorite in this little town that's a quick trip from San Antonio gives you a trip back in time — to 1952, in fact, the year the cafe opened. The kind of place that offers the cooking Grandma used to make after church on Sunday, it's where you go to feel coddled and, well, comforted. Take someone along who loves cream gravy.

In the know: Cypress Creek offers a popular lunch buffet weekdays and homey specials on Sunday. Comfort is one of those places you go to escape the modern world and find a real sense of peace and quiet. The High Street that runs the length of its quaint downtown is lined with shops and galleries and a few B&B inns.

Picks: Chicken-fried steak, meatloaf, roast beef, pork chops, turkey and dressing, house-made pies.

Details: Lunch Tue-Sun; dinner Wed-Sat. BYOB.

Friesenhaus Restaurant and Bakery
148 S. Castell Ave., New Braunfels
830-625-1040, friesenhausnb.com

Why go: When you're craving solid German cooking, this is your destination, right in the heart of purely German New Braunfels. Operated for nearly 70 years as Krause's Cafe, this happy, sprawling place serves specialties from Bavaria, Rhineland, Berlin and the North Sea.

In the know: Make a day of it and explore the German heritage museums, then cool off on the slides and chutes at Schlitterbahn or go for a float on the Comal River in the city park. Wind down with a relaxing evening in the Friesenhaus beer garden, where dogs and smokers are welcome.

Picks: Sauerbraten, wienerschnitzel, potato soup, German sausage salad, fresh breads and pastries are recommended. Look also for traditional German sausage and cheese plates and a good tea selection, plus a broad range of German beers and wines.

Details: Lunch and dinner daily. Full bar.

Gristmill River Restaurant & Bar
1287 Gruene Road, New Braunfels
830-625-0684, gristmillrestaurant.com

Why go: A favorite stop since 1977 in the village of Gruene (pronounced "Green"), on the Guadalupe River at the north end of New Braunfels, the Gristmill draws enormous crowds, especially on weekends and almost any day in summer. Folks come to Gruene in droves to float on rafts or inner tubes along the Guadalupe and to hear live music next door at historic Gruene Hall, the state's oldest dance hall in continuous use. The restaurant unfolds within an old mill with soaring rock walls, and decks offer a leafy view of the river.

In the know: Hit town early so you can shop the boutiques, antique shops, galleries and wine-tasting rooms before lunch or dinner. The Gristmill often offers music on the patio, where you're likely to wait a while for a dinner table — but the beer is cold and margaritas are pretty good, so you'll have fun while cooling your heels.

Picks: Burgers and steaks are top choices; salads and quesadillas are popular, as well. Tomatillo chicken is among the popular entrees.

Details: Lunch and dinner daily. Full bar.

Health Camp

2601 Circle Road, Waco
254-752-2186
health-camp-waco.com

Why go: Opened in 1949 on one of the more treacherous traffic circles in the state, just west of I-35 (take the Valley Mill exit), this old drive-in has been a legend for longer that most of us can remember. Be assured that there is absolutely nothing healthy about the food here, but it's mighty tasty. It reminds us of the old-school burger hangouts that used to be found in almost every Texas town.

In the know: Buy a T-shirt that claims "I survived the Circle!" Be sure to check out the historic photos around the dining room.

Picks: Cheeseburgers, chili dogs, fries, tater tots, handmade shakes and custard ice cream in a multitude of flavors keep loyal customers happy.

Details: Lunch and dinner daily. No bar.

Kreuz Market

619 N. Colorado St., Lockhart
512-398-2361, kreuzmarket.com

Why go: The founding family's original meat market and grocery store opened in 1900, and the barbecue joint as we know it opened nearly 50 years later. Kreuz (pronounced "Krites") sat for many years on the Lockhart square but moved — after a family feud that split the business into two barbecue places — to this much larger and more comfortable (if less atmospheric) space in 1999. In this vast, hangar-like newer location, you can get side dishes such as beans, German potato salad and sauerkraut, but you still order at the source — the smoky pit room. And you still won't find barbecue sauce (the meat is so flavorful and smoky you don't need it), forks or plates (butcher paper works just fine).

In the know: Occupying the original location on the square is Smitty's, also still very popular for the traditional smoked 'cue for which this part of the state is famous.

Picks: Beef shoulder clod, beef brisket, pork ribs, jalapeño sausage and beef prime rib are all super-smoky and really good.

Details: Lunch and dinner Mon-Sat; closed Sun. Beer.

Louie Mueller Barbecue
206 W. Second St., Taylor
512-352-6206, louiemuellerbarbecue.com

Why go: Found about an hour northeast of Austin, the 1949-vintage legend shows you its worth in its walls. Deeply stained with decades of wood smoke, this gem is a complete throwback to another age, when food stores also doubled as places to eat. One of *Texas Monthly*'s favorite places, Louie Mueller will become yours, too, as you embrace its venerable heritage. The barbecue is still served on butcher paper by folks who have had the art of smoking meat over post-oak fires in their veins for generations.

In the know: If you arrive at peak lunch hour, you'll be standing in line, but you can enjoy a cold drink to help you endure the wait. While you're waiting for the meat cutter to pile the exceptional meats on your tray, he'll toss a dark and crusty little burnt end of brisket (that's a really good thing) on your tray for you to nibble on as you move through the cafeteria-style service. And if you're coming from out of town and are worried your favorite cuts might sell out, you can call ahead and place your order.

Picks: Sliced or chopped, the beef brisket is magnificent, as is the beef rib, which is massive. Pork ribs are excellent, too, and so is the jalapeño sausage. Sides of beans and potato salad are just fine, and peach cobbler is the perfect finish.

Details: Lunch and early dinner Mon-Sat; closed Sun. Beer.

Maxine'sCafe
905 Main St., Bastrop
512-303-0919, maxinescafe.com

Why go: Stationed toward one end of bustling Main Street in this charming and fast-growing town on the Colorado River, Maxine's serves as a hub of activity in Bastrop. It's packed at breakfast on the weekends and nearly any hour of the lunch and dinner service. In the afternoons, a group of guitar pickers may converge just when you've stopped in for a piece of the legendary pie. Weekends, you can expect live-music shows, along with a jovial crowd.

In the know: If you're motoring through Bastrop, you can grab fresh breads, pastries and pies on the fly at Maxine's catering and bakery operation, 1507 Chestnut St. (512-412-6090). There's also a Maxine's in Elgin.

Picks: Breakfast joys include eggs Florentine, which piles an English muffin with fresh spinach, Canadian bacon, poached egg and hollandaise; and the famous griddle cake, a 12-inch pancake that can be enhanced with blueberry, chocolate-chip, pecan-praline or apple-cinnamon mix-ins. For lunch and dinner, we like the fried pickle spears with chipotle ranch dressing, fried green tomato BLT, chicken pot pie, pot roast and a piece of butterscotch pie for dessert.

Details: Breakfast and lunch daily; dinner Tue-Sat. Beer and wine.

Monument Cafe
500 S. Austin Ave., Georgetown
512-930-9586, themonumentcafe.com

Why go: Though it's a relative newcomer — it opened in 1995 and moved to its current home in 2008 — the Monument Cafe's charm is that it evokes the feeling of a vintage coffee shop, in food, service and atmosphere, with its curvy glass-block retro-diner look. It's a good place to fill up, morning through evening.

In the know: If you want to stick around Georgetown for a little while, visit the beautiful Southwestern University campus and the pretty courthouse square downtown.

Picks: Huevos rancheros and eggs with chicken-fried steak are good at breakfast; chili, Cobb salad and burgers make for a tasty lunch; and King Ranch casserole, enchiladas and pan-fried pork chops are popular dinner choices. Chocolate pie, with a toasted-pecan crust, is always good, too.

Details: Breakfast, lunch and dinner daily. Beer and wine.

Royer's Cafe
105 Main St., Round Top
979-249-3611, royersroundtopcafe.com

Why go: Though it's been open since 1946, this tiny cafe in the exceptionally tiny town of Round Top has become wildly popular in more recent years for its truly remarkable pies. Bud Royer, whose food and story have been featured in a number of magazines and even on a CBS morning show, has built a lofty reputation for his contemporary comfort food. The menu is shameless fun, with lots of dishes noted as "OMG!" delicious.

In the know: Count on OMG! crowds on weekends, when the wait can be two hours for a table at high noon or prime dinner time. And if you can't live without Royer's pies, note that they are shipped everywhere – and they make wonderful gifts. Royer's now has a pie shop in Austin, too.

Picks: Grilled shrimp BLT, pork tenderloin, steaks, soups and salads all get high marks. But the pies are what you'll dream about. Our favorite is the multi-berry pie.

Details: Lunch Wed-Sun; dinner Thu-Sat. Beer and wine.

Snow's BBQ
516 Main St., Lexington
979-542-8189, snowsbbq.com

Why go: Operating in relative quiet until *Texas Monthly* discovered the place and then national media came calling, Snow's is unusual on two accounts. First, it's only open on Saturday. Second, its pitmaster is the rarest of all breeds – a woman. Tootsie Tomanetz knows her stuff, and though she's in her late 70s, we think she'll be going strong for quite some time yet.

In the know: The lines here can be insane, so you should plan to arrive by 9 a.m. on Saturday to make sure you get to taste all the goods. Chances are, Snow's will sell out of most everything by noon or shortly thereafter. Even if you're standing in line, you'll be in good company with the tourists from everywhere coming to eat some of the finest barbecue ever served. Everyone sits at community tables under a metal shed.

Picks: From Tootsie's post-oak pits come beef brisket, pork ribs, pork steak (a cut from the pig's shoulder) and pork-and-beef sausage. Solid sides include pinto beans and potato salad. The pecan pie is excellent, too.

Details: Lunch Sat. BYOB.

Stagecoach Inn

416 S. Main St., Salado
254-947-5111, stagecoachsalado.com

Why go: Open since the mid 1800s, this historic inn reopened its restaurant after a year-long renovation that bought long-overdue updates. The historic charm was left intact, and the new owners hired a culinary team to put new spins on the restaurant's classics.

In the know: The inn remains in business, with massive remodeling bringing the rooms to modern comfort and style demands. If you decide to spend time in Salado, there are lots of B&B inns, too, as well as plentiful antiques shops and nice walks along Salado Creek. Check out the local museum, which gives a good look at the history of Scottish settlers in Texas.

Picks: Hushpuppies, chicken-fried steak, deep-fried bacon with onion jam and Texas toast, tomahawk pork chop with black-eyed peas and slow-smoked beer can chicken are among stars on the new menu. The Strawberry Kiss remains the signature dessert. Cocktails are among new additions, too; try the hibiscus margarita.

Details: Credit cards. Lunch and dinner, Wed-Sun. Full bar.

Sunset Grill

902 S. Adams St., Fredericksburg
830-997-5904

Why go: The locals will tell you, this is the go-to for great food at breakfast and lunch. It's blessedly off the heavy tourist traffic path, so there's no trouble with parking — but that doesn't mean there won't be a wait for a table. The café spreads out within an old cottage and its pretty patio.

In the know: Everything on the menu satisfies, but the daily specials are always exceptional. These range from Mediterranean shrimp pasta with artichokes in a white wine sauce to Hangtown Bennie, fried oysters with poached eggs, bacon, sautéed spinach, pico de gallo and hollandaise sauce.

Picks: The smoked salmon Benedict, oyster po'boy, fried zucchini, black and blue burger and caramelized banana French toast are among favorites.

Details: Breakfast and lunch, Thu-Tue. Credit cards. Beer and wine.

Wenzel Lonestar Meat Co.
209 N. Bell St., Hamilton
254-386-8242, wenzellonestarmeat.com

Why go: A meat market with offerings that include bison, beef, sausages, triple-smoked bacon and more, this place doubles as a great little lunch spot. You'll find it one block off the Hamilton County square, with excellent signage out front.

In the know: It's busy at lunchtime, so plan an early or late visit or be prepared to wait for one of the few tables. In addition to meat-market offerings and lunch goods, there's plenty of merchandise to peruse, including jars of pickled okra, mango-lime salsa, pepper sauce, meat rubs, T-shirts, hats and bumper stickers with the signature "Bite My Butt" slogan, referring to the famous pork butt smoked and served here.

Picks: When the lunch counter is open, huge deli sandwiches are offered. Peppered beef with hot-pepper cheddar and spicy mustard is outstanding; you can have it served warm or cold. On the first Monday of each month, the bison bacon burger is the special. On Wednesday, the whole stuffed smoked baked potato— the "greater tater" — is your choice. On Fridays, it's a pork butt sandwich, a massive barbecue undertaking.

Details: Lunch Mon-Sat; closed Sun. No bar.

Woerner Warehouse
305 S. Lincoln St., Fredericksburg
830-997-2246, woernerwarehouse.com

Why go: Inside an old feed store awaits some of the best food to be offered in the Hill Country in quite some time. It's not fancy, but it's certainly of great quality, and the service comes with big, genuine smiles, too.

In the know: The cafe also sells locally sourced jams, jellies and coffees, as well as pasture-raised lamb, chicken and farm-fresh eggs. Next door, one of the finest antiques stores in Central Texas — Carol Hicks Bolton Antiqüités — begs exploration. Do yourself a favor and wander through. New shipments arrive from France periodically.

Picks: Picks: An overhauled menu offers pizzas (the Works includes pepperoni, salami, onion, olives, artichoke hearts, mozzarella and tomato sauce); panini (the Don Juan comes with ham, bacon, house slaw, tomato, onion, dill havarti, Dijon mayo on grilled sourdough); and salads (the house special combines spinach, Gorgonzola, sun dried pears, red onion, and candied pecans).

Details: Credit cards. Lunch Mon-Sat; dinner Fri-Sat. Beer and wine.

East Texas

BBQ Express
801 Elmore St., Marshall
903-923-8705

Why go: You'll have to wander off the beaten path to find this gem, an easy-to-miss spot in a residential area. It's well worth your effort, as Herbert and Patrice White have worked hard to bring excellent barbecue together with soul food, providing a solid Southern eating experience.

In the know: To find it, look for the small business sitting at the corner of Elysian Fields Road and Elmore Street. It's just west of U.S. 59, the main north-south thoroughfare running through Marshall.

Picks: Brisket is a huge favorite, but the ribs — falling-off-the-bone tender — are outstanding. Deviled eggs and barbecue beans are exceptional, too. For some righteous soul food, try the collard greens and cornbread.

Details: Lunch and early dinner, Tue-Sun. No bar.

Big Pines Lodge

747 Pine Island Road, Karnack
903-679-3655, bigpineslodge.com

Why go: Open since 1953, Big Pines Lodge rebuilt a few years ago after a huge fire, and it's far nicer than ever before. You can arrive by boat at a big dock, if you like. It's definitely a big, friendly family place, with lots of alligator motif in the decor; Caddo Lake here is known for its 'gator population.

In the know: The restaurant sits within easy reach of Caddo Lake State Park, one of the most beautiful natural areas in Texas. On pretty spring, summer and fall weekends, you can bet on finding a big crowd here, especially for the groaning-board Sunday brunch. On "Thrifty Tuesdays," from 5 to 8 p.m., it's all-you-can-eat catfish and fixin's.

Picks: Order catfish and you'll find a giant mound of crispy fried fillets set before you. You can also order alligator tail, another fried specialty, as well as a monster basket of hushpuppies. Don't pass up the green-tomato relish, an East Texas specialty.

Details: Breakfast Sat-Sun; lunch Wed-Sun (brunch buffet Sun); dinner Tue-Sun; closed Mon. Beer and wine.

Country Tavern Bar-B-Que

Texas 31 at Farm Road 2767, Kilgore
903-984-9954

Why go: Open since 1939, this roadhouse is a family-friendly spot — if your kids don't mind a crowd that gets a little lively as the evening wears on. It's a legendary destination in these parts, so don't be surprised if you have to wait for a table at prime eating time.

In the know: Don't look for a menu; just read the blackboard when you walk in. It tells you about all the barbecue and sides that are offered. When you get messy from all those ribs, there are hot towels to clean your hands and face.

Picks: Ribs, first and foremost, are what bring folks into the Country Tavern. The meat slides right off the bone, and that's the way customers like it. Other picks include sliced brisket, turkey and jalapeño sausage. Among sides, baked-potato casserole is a specialty.

Details: Lunch and dinner Mon-Sat. Full bar.

The Diner
7924 S. Broadway Ave., Tyler
903-509-3463, thedinertyler.com

Why go: While not vintage in the least, this shopping-center cafe does a good job of bringing old-fashioned ideas into contemporary presentations. It's a friendly place with a wide selection of American vittles, some with a healthy diet in mind.

In the know: This place sits in the south end of town, not far from a newish toll road that makes travel to points south from I-20 far easier than in the past.

Picks: Appetizers include fried dill pickle chips and bacon-cheese fries, but you can be healthy with a fresh fruit plate. Fried green tomatoes are a big hit here, as are fried chicken, roasted brisket in brown gravy and spinach quiche. At breakfast, you can be virtuous with a veggie egg-white frittata or go wild with a chicken-fried steak omelet or cinnamon-roll pancakes. Quiches and casseroles like King Ranch chicken are a specialty, and you can order whole ones, which they'll even bake in your own dish if you want.

Details: Breakfast and lunch daily. No bar.

Excelsior House

211 W. Austin St., Jefferson
903-665-2513, theexcelsiorhouse.com

Why go: Open since 1858 and one of the oldest, most-loved inns in all the South, the Excelsior is among a vanishing breed of graceful places where you don't have to be rich to feel welcome. Famous guests who have stayed here include Ulysses Grant, Oscar Wilde and Lady Bird Johnson, the latter having grown up nearby. Breakfast is the big daily event at the Excelsior, where the dining room usually requires a reservation in advance.

In the know: The town is packed on weekends during the Christmas season, Mardi Gras and the annual spring Pilgrimage, with its Old South Ball, so book early.

Picks: The lavish breakfast is known for its orange-blossom muffins; don't pass these up.

Details: Breakfast Friday-Sunday. Credit cards. No bar. (Groups of 8 or more may reserve breakfast during the week.)

Hickory House

801 Elmore St., Marshall
903-923-8705

Why go: You'll have to wander off the beaten path to find this gem, an easy-to-miss spot in a residential area. It's well worth your effort, as Herbert and Patrice White have worked hard to bring excellent barbecue together with soul food, providing a solid Southern eating experience.

In the know: To find it, look for the small business sitting at the corner of Elysian Fields Road and Elmore Street. It's just west of U.S. 59, the main north-south thoroughfare running through Marshall.

Picks: Sides are never an afterthought here; get the fried mushrooms, squash and onion rings.

Details: Lunch and early dinner, Tue-Sun. Credit cards. No bar.

Jucys Hamburgers
2701 N. Eastman Rd., Longview
903-758-9056, jucyshamburgers.com

Why go: Opening its first doors in Longview back in 1980, this beloved burger restaurant now boasts six locations, found in Longview, Marshall and Tyler. Fresh preparations mean a lot to the ownership, as beef is ground daily on-site at each place and fries are freshly cut from russet potatoes every morning.

In the know: Readers of *Texas Highways* magazine voted this the best burger in Texas in 2015. And the sister company, Jucys Taco, has three locations in Longview, as well.

Picks: The burger topped with blue cheese and bacon is a sure hit, and the burger blanketed in melted Cheddar and grilled onions is hard to beat. But don't overlook that beautiful chicken-fried steak.

Details: Lunch and dinner, daily. (Two locations are open at 6 a.m., too.) Credit cards. No bar.

Mike's Barbeque House
1622 South St., Nacogdoches
936-560-1676, mikesbarbequehouse.net

Why go: If no-frills Southern barbecue is your quest, this is the place. Very down-home, Mike's serves its 'cue on paper plates with plastic ware.

In the know: Mike's is just a little south of Stephen F. Austin State University, so it's a good place to eat if you're visiting the campus.

Picks: One of the unusual offerings is a chopped brisket sandwich that adds a chopped sausage into the works, with sauce, on a big bun. The potato salad is the mustard variety, and there are jalapeños stuffed with pimiento cheese if you need a little zip on the side. Stuffed baked potatoes make for a giant meal, but you'll want to leave room for blackberry cobbler.

Details: Lunch and dinner daily. No bar.

Pickett House
157 Private Road 6000, Woodville
409-283-3371, heritage-village.org/pickett-house.htm

Why go: Opened in 1965, this very old-fashioned restaurant sits inside a restored country home that's part of Heritage Village, a "living history" re-creation of a pioneer village off U.S. 190 deep in the Piney Woods. The boarding-house-style service takes you back at least a century into the past.

In the know: This is a good lunch-break spot if you're touring Heritage Village or if you've just finished a big hike or early-morning canoe trip at Big Thicket National Preserve, which lies about 30 minutes due south of Woodville.

Picks: Fried chicken remains the most popular choice, served with mashed potatoes, barbecue beans, stewed greens and cornbread. The pickle bar stocks watermelon rind, a real Southern treat, as well as beets and jalapeños. There's peach cobbler for dessert, too.

Details: Lunch daily; early supper Sat-Sun. No bar.

Pittsburg Hot Links Restaurant
136 Marshall St., Pittsburg
903-856-5765, pittsburghotlink.com

Why go: A delicacy from exactly this part of the state is the hot link, created in the late 1800s by a German settler. This somewhat spicy sausage made from beef and pork is a dark red in color, and it's a specialty at this restaurant, where the old custom is to eat the links with saltines and hot sauce.

In the know: You can order the links online, too, from the restaurant's website. There's a hot-link eating contest held here each year in September.

Picks: Service is cafeteria-style, and everyone sits at long community tables. In addition to the sausage links, you can find Frito pie, chili, corn dogs, fried okra, hamburgers and jalapeño cornbread.

Details: Breakfast, lunch and early dinner Mon-Sat; closed Sun. No bar.

The Shed Cafe
8337 Farm Road 279, Edom
903-852-7791, theshedcafe.com

Why go: Open since 1966, this old-fashioned favorite sitting in the wide spot of a country road draws people all the way from Dallas and Shreveport in the middle of the week, just to have lunch. The home-style cooking has become legendary, as has the simple country atmosphere.

In the know: It's just a short drive east of Canton, so plan to visit during your First Monday shopping trip. Tuesday nights bring "Pickin' and Grinnin'," a popular country jam session.

Picks: Have eggs cooked any way you like with pork chops or a steak at breakfast. At lunch and dinner, there's chef salad, chicken-fried steak, catfish and more. The pies bring people in droves, so save room for dessert.

Details: Breakfast, lunch and dinner daily. No bar.

Stanley's Famous Pit Bar-B-Q
525 S. Beckham Ave., Tyler
903-593-0311, stanleysfamous.com

Why go: Though Stanley's is more than a half-century old, there's a hipness imparted by a youthful ownership that makes the place seem contemporary. The 'cue is Central Texas-style in woodsmoke flavor, and the live music and craft cocktail scene bring Austin venues to mind.

In the know: Be prepared to stand in line at peak lunch and dinner hours, because this place is so darn good. That's OK, because once you grab a table — preferably on the open-air deck — you can linger over your food and drinks, soaking in the atmosphere. Wednesday happy hour brings great drink specials.

Picks: Baby back ribs are rubbed in 11 spices and served in a delightfully saucy mess. Smoke turkey is a big, wonderful surprise, and handmade sausage from a local maker is another must. At breakfast, you have to try JD's Bowl, a layering of scrambled eggs with pan-fried potatoes, a choice of meat (get either brisket or pulled pork) and cheddar cheese.

Details: Breakfast, Mon-Fri; lunch and early dinner, Mon-Sat. Credit cards. Full bar.

Gulf Coast

Avery's Kitchen
200 W. Ave. G, Port Aransas
361-749-0650

Why go: Avery's is probably the busiest place on Mustang Island at breakfast, and you'll know the reason as soon as you tuck into a big plate of goodness. It's definitely not fancy, but the warm welcome everyone gets makes this an instant favorite.

In the know: About midway between beach and bay, this spot is convenient to nearly everything in Port A. If there's a big fishing tournament in town, it may be especially crowded. A number of Avery's specialties originated at the Dockside Bar & Grill, where owner Avery Hernandez cooked for 15 years before opening his own place.

Picks: The huevos rancheros come with eggs cooked any style, and the Hungry Fisherman's Breakfast packs a punch with biscuits or toast, hash browns or grits, two eggs any style and a thick ham steak. At lunch and dinner, choose from chopped sirloin steak, chicken-fried steak, fried shrimp or oysters, homemade crab cake and po'boy sandwiches. Avery's wife makes the key lime pie.

Details: Cash only.

Cafe Michael Burger
11150 FM 3005, Galveston
409-740-3639, cafemichaelburger.com

Why go: With more than two decades in business, this madly popular burger joint is a favorite among beach folks and has outlasted a lot of competition. The burger has won statewide mention from *Texas Monthly*.

In the know: The German owner brings a whole 'nother flavor to the menu, making this more than a burger joint: Order from the roster of schnitzel and wurst dishes, if you like, and give the house-made strudel a try.

Picks: Purists pick the Michael Burger, a third-of-a-pounder with the usual trimmings; the Tiki Burger adds sautéed mushrooms, onion, Swiss cheese and mayo, with a wheat bun. The Jamaica Beach Burger offers grilled pineapple, jalapeño and Swiss; and the Lichtenfeldt sports sauerkraut, Swiss and spicy German mustard. There are also hot dogs and Reuben and schnitzel-on-rye sandwiches.

Details: Lunch and dinner Wed-Sun; closed Mon-Tue. Beer and wine.

The Cafe on the Beach
3616 Gulf Blvd., South Padre Island
956-761-1316, palmsresortcafe.com

Why go: Though this island is packed with places to eat, few are on the beach. The Palms Resort's restaurant is one of that select few, with an intimate feel to boot – there are fewer than a dozen tables. You can see the ocean, and you're next to the pool serving the resort's guests.

In the know: It's crowded on a pretty weekend, but in the off season you'll have the place to yourself — or you'll share it with the winter Texans. Note the house rules that say, "No smoking; no whining children, adults or animals."

Picks: Eggs Benedict, corned beef hash, raisin French toast and malted pancakes are among morning specialties, as well as smoked salmon with cream cheese, capers and a bagel. At lunch and dinner, great choices include shrimp cocktail, steamed mussels, seafood bisque, a super-healthy raw-veggie salad, blackened-shrimp tacos, grilled red snapper and lobster tail. The menu is huge.

Details: Breakfast, lunch and dinner daily. Full bar.

Gaido's Seafood Restaurant
3828 Seawall Blvd., Galveston
409-762-9625, gaidos.com

Why go: Open since 1911 and still family-run, Gaido's doesn't exactly fit into our cafe definition, but you can't talk about Texas' classic restaurants without including this place. Homemade recipes for sauces, salad dressings and soups have been on the menu for all time, and service comes from the old school, with waiters wearing little ties. White linens are on the table, and prices are not cheap, but it's not at all fancy.

In the know: Possibly the best-known restaurant on the coast, Gaido's tends to stay busy; aim for an off-peak hour and ask for a table with a view of the Gulf. It was big news in Galveston recently when Gaido's exclusive Pelican Club, formerly members-only, hired its own chef and began offering an adventurous fine-dining menu to the public.

Picks: The soup sampler includes shrimp bisque and gumbo, and the baked-oyster combo platter is good, as are cracker-crusted red snapper and charbroiled scallops with au gratin potatoes. The crab dishes are popular, and Key lime pie and pecan pie are fine dessert choices.

Details: Lunch and dinner daily. Full bar.

King's Inn
1116 E. County Road 2270, Baffin Bay
361-297-5265

Why go: Since 1945, this restaurant has been a favorite in its out-of-the-way spot on Loyola Beach in the Coastal Plains area, southeast of Kingsville. Its trademarks are family-style meals and a menu that's recited by the servers (there's no printed menu, and you order by the pound).

In the know: Some 30,000 pounds of seafood is served here annually. It continues to be popular — guests have included visiting royalty from abroad, as well as Nolan Ryan and the occasional movie star — so you'll want to make reservations; otherwise, expect a long wait. This is a good stop if you're traveling down U.S. 77 from Corpus Christi to the Rio Grande Valley.

Picks: Fried shrimp, oysters, onion rings, French fries and avocado salad are the most popular orders; grilled black drum is recommended, and the restaurant is famous for its spicy tartar sauce, which it sells to take home.

Details: Lunch and dinner Tue-Sat; closed Sun-Mon. No bar.

Leon's World's Finest In and Out BBQ House
5427 Broadway, Galveston
409-744-0070, leonsbbq.com

Why go: With more than a quarter-century under its belt, Leon's serves excellent barbecue from an old house right on the island's main drag. It consistently ranks among the state's best in respected polls.

In the know: Like a lot of the best barbecue joints, it's really a lunchtime place. So if you're spending a day on the beach, plan your lunch around a quick side trip to Leon's.

Picks: Choices among sandwiches include prime beef brisket, North Carolina BBQ, ribs, link sausage and sliced smoked turkey. Side dishes show Southern/soul food influences, such as spicy rice and turnip greens. There's boudin, if you're craving Cajun, and cracklin's, too. For dessert, try rum cake, buttermilk pie or sweet potato pie.

Details: Lunch daily; early dinner Fri-Sun. Beer.

Rosie's Soul Food
2306 Hazel Ave., Beaumont
409-832-7685, rosiessoulfood.com

Why go: Home-cooking and family-owned, this unassuming spot in serves meals cafeteria-style, and the portions are huge. Most guests find themselves taking home half their meal for next-day lunch.

In the know: While Rosie's may seem out of the way, it's tucked into Beaumont's Old Town District, close to the I-10/U.S. 69 exchange, and about halfway between the Babe Zaharias Memorial Stadium and the McFaddin-Ward House Historic Museum.

Picks: Braised oxtails, fried chicken, meatloaf and baked chicken with rice are favorite entrees, while old-fashioned greens, lima beans, corn and cornbread are sides of choice.

Details: Lunch and dinner daily (early closing Sat-Sun). No bar.

Sartin's Seafood
3520 Nederland Ave., Nederland
409-721-9420, sartins.com

Why go: A regional legend since the early 1970s, Sartin's has had a number of locations in and around the Beaumont area. This one, close to Port Arthur, is the latest spot that draws crowds to dig into a righteous delicacy known as barbecued crabs.

In the know: They're not really barbecued — they're coated with a spicy Cajun seasoning rub and then deep-fried — but the crabs *are* messy, so if you're trying to be dainty or impress someone, please lose that desire. Just eat these and use lots of napkins.

Picks: First and foremost, you have to try the barbecued crabs. There's nothing like these – anywhere. Stuffed crab balls are mighty fine, too. Blue-plate specials include shrimp Creole and crawfish.

Details: Lunch and dinner Mon-Sat; lunch only Sun. Beer and wine.

Snoopy's Pier
13313 S. Padre Island Drive, Corpus Christi
361-949-8815, snoopyspier.com

Why go: Opened in 1980, this is a sort of Jimmy-Buffett-style place. There's probably not a more laid-back and rustic fish joint on the coast, and you can come by car or boat. Sitting right on the Intracoastal Canal under the causeway that leads to Padre Island National Seashore, Snoopy's catches great breezes on its open-air decks. In winter, you can sit inside by the fireplace.

In the know: It's almost always busy, so go early or late. And don't dress up – shorts and flip-flops are perfect.

Picks: Sandwiches include fried shrimp or oyster with curly fries or hush puppies; dinners range from deviled crab plate to shrimp creole to fried-fish platters. There are burgers and cold beer, too.

Details: Lunch and dinner daily. Cash only. Beer and wine.

Sonny's Place

1206 19th St., Galveston
409- 763-9602, galveston.com/sonnys

Why go: Opened in the 1940s by the Puccetti family — one of dozens of Italian families to launch restaurants on Galveston Island — this decidedly dated and downscale joint is one of the island's true institutions. The food is pretty cheap and good, the service is surly in a good-natured way and the beer is ice-cold.

In the know: In addition to locals, medical students keep this place hopping.

Picks: Ask for the oyster mug, an off-the-menu special that packs lots of freshly shucked oysters into an icy mug with plenty of cocktail sauce. The shrimp bun is a favorite, as is the muffaletta, the cheeseburger and spaghetti with meat sauce.

Details: Lunch and dinner Tue-Sat; closed Sun-Mon. Beer and wine.

Southside Barbacoa

5894 Everhart Rd., Corpus Christi
361-334-0888

Why go: "Authentic" is putting it lightly — this is the real thing, if you're in search of true Mexican food. Speaking Spanish is helpful but not altogether necessary. Small and clean, it's on a busy corner with a homemade, family-friendly vibe.

In the know: Carne guisada tacos are the Saturday morning specialty, and barbacoa is the Sunday morning choice. There's a local band that plays nearby on weekends, so you'll have music with breakfast.

Picks: In addition to the mentions above, look for homestyle omelets, eggs cooked as you like with bacon and the best handmade flour tortillas ever, pancakes and delicious, fruit-filled empanadas. To drink? If not coffee or tea, try the Big Red.

Details: Breakfast and lunch, Tue-Sun. Credit cards. No bar.

Stingaree
1295 N. Stingaree Road, Crystal Beach
409-684-2731, tingareerestaurant.com

Why go: Rebuilt after Hurricane Ike paid its savage visit to Galveston environs in 2008, this big, convivial, laid-back spot easily ranks as one of the best seafood houses in the Galveston region. Sitting on the Bolivar Peninsula, just a short ferry ride from Galveston Island, Stingaree has been keeping locals and visitors profoundly happy.

In the know: With its ideal perch over the water on the intracoastal canal, you can catch some very impressive sunsets on the balcony while you eat dinner or just sip a beer or "Stingarita." Watch the restaurant's Facebook page to find out when live-music acts are booked.

Picks: French-grilled local oysters, lump crab sautéed in basil-laced butter, wild Gulf shrimp with a honey-jalapeño treatment and specials like Oysters Jubilee for two (a panoply of oyster specialties served in three courses) set Stingaree apart from most coastal seafood places. For a taste of Louisiana, there's gumbo, barbecued blue crabs from Galveston Bay and boudin balls.

Details: Lunch and dinner daily. Full bar.

Swinging Door

3818 Farm Road 359, Richmond
281-342-4758, swingingdoor.com

Why go: Opened in 1973, the Door is part dance hall and part barbecue joint, and it seems to have been created by Hollywood as the quintessential Texas roadhouse. Popular with regulars and private parties, this big yellow barn-like building is almost always buzzing.

In the know: This is one of the Texas barbecue places that will ship its wares, so you can enjoy the 'cue back home, too.

Picks: Smoked over pecan embers, the barbecue includes beef brisket, pork ribs, chicken, sausage and turkey breast. A loaded baked potato can be topped with any of those meats, and there are beans, dirty rice and potato salad among side choices. Fruit cobbler is best for dessert.

Details: Lunch and dinner Wed-Sun. Beer and wine.

Willy Burger

5535 Calder Ave., Beaumont
409-892-3400, willy-burger.com

Why go: Included on *Texas Monthly*'s list of the 50 best burgers in Texas, this upstart feels comfortably vintage, thanks to the Airstream out front and the 1960s graphics that bring *The Jetsons* to mind. The food is very modern, though, in design and ingredietns.

In the know: The reason the burgers taste so good is the due largely to the high-quality product. The kitchen grinds its 100 percent certified Angus chuck daily and shapes each patty by hand. Want something a bit healthier? There's grilled tuna steak option, and a gluten-free bun for any sandwich.

Picks: In addition to beautiful, towering burgers, there's the Fred Sanford, a fried pork chop sandwich; a Kung Fu burger loaded with Asian slaw, bacon strips, jalapenos and pepper jack cheese; and a bowl of good ol' Texas chili. Slap a fried egg on anything, if you like. And get a Coke float for dessert.

Details: Lunch and dinner daily. Credit cards. Beer and wine.

North Texas

Babe's Chicken Dinner House

104 N. Oak St., Roanoke
817-491-2900, babeschicken.com

Why go: Popular almost since the doors were opened in 1993, the original shop in the growing Babe's fried-chicken empire occupies a century-old building in a tiny downtown in southern Denton County. Babe's is filled with old wooden chairs and tables, and its walls are hung with faded signs. Servers are known to break into the hokey-pokey between deliveries of massive, family-style platters of chicken and all the sides you can handle.

In the know: There's always a wait for tables at peak hours, and some guests bring camp chairs and coolers to keep them comfortable while waiting on the sidewalk. Since 2008, multiple other locations have opened in places such as Burleson, Frisco, Granbury, Arlington and Cedar Hill.

Picks: At the original Babe's, your choices are fried chicken and chicken-fried steak. At some of the larger locations, you can order roasted chicken, pot roast and other entrees. Mashed potatoes and creamed corn are the popular sides. Big biscuits, served with sorghum syrup, are a true indulgence.

Details: Lunch and dinner daily. BYOB.

Bar L Drive Inn
908 13th St., Wichita Falls
940-761-3990

Why go: Unchanged since its opening in 1951, this is both a true drive-in and a dive. As long as you go knowing that it's very, very old-school, and nobody prissy is in your party, you'll be fine. Smoking is still allowed, but this place is comforting in its purely yesteryear way. On a hot day, it's heavenly and cool inside.

In the know: If it's a nice day outside, get carhop service and enjoy that rarity while it lasts. Sometimes bands set up on weekends and party down.

Picks: Pork ribs, garlic-steak sandwich and the burger are all good. The Red Draw is the cold beer of choice.

Details: Lunch and dinner daily. Beer and wine.

Catfish Plantation
814 Water St., Waxahachie
972-937-9468, catfishplantation.com

Why go: The cute 1895 house that's housed this restaurant for decades was reopened after a fire in 2003. Though the restaurant changed hands in 2007, it remains a popular place for a destination lunch or dinner.

In the know: To suggest the home is haunted is an understatement; the stories are legendary and have been featured on numerous TV programs. Nevertheless, it's a great place to eat. On Thursday and Sunday evenings, check out the all-you-can-eat options. Seniors get a 15 percent discount; if you have a group of eight or more, ask for the family-style dinner.

Picks: Fried catfish, naturally, is the big draw, but entrée choices also include chicken and dumplings, chicken-fried steak, popcorn shrimp and lemon-pepper tilapia.

Details: Lunch Thu-Sun; dinner Wed-Sun; closed Mon-Tue. Beer and wine.

The Center Restaurant & Tavern
603 E. U.S. 82, Muenster
940-759-2910, thecenterrestaurant.com

Why go: If you thought all the German heritage in Texas was found in the Hill Country and San Antonio, you were wrong. Just west of Gainesville and near the Red River, you'll find Muenster, a community rich in German spirit. At its heart is the 1950s-vintage Center, a big, happy place where German food and atmosphere are served generously.

In the know: The main dining room is more traditional and quiet; the tavern usually has a game on TV, while the expansive outdoor biergarten has picnic tables and a bandstand for live entertainment on weekends. The last weekend in April is Muensterfest, which guarantees the town will be packed.

Picks: Schnitzels, sausages and other traditional goods, including Reubens, strudel and steaks, are popular.

Details: Breakfast, lunch and dinner Tue-Sun; closed Mon. Full bar.

Del Norte Tacos
101 E. Highway 171, Godley
817-389-2451, delnortetacos.com

Why go: This tiny ranching town south of Fort Worth has become a destination for people who know what good food awaits them here. Inside an old rock building, chef Chris Garcia presents sensational plates of food in a casual setting.

In the know: Every Friday and Saturday evening, there's live music on stage. Folks gather at big picnic tables in the open-air patio.

Picks: The fajita taco and the blackened fish taco are simply wonderful, and for the vegetarian, there's one with avocado, black beans, cheese, slaw and cilantro. Besides tacos, the menu includes a great chopped barbecue beef sandwich, enchiladas, smoked chile relleno and a full barbecue plate with sides. Blackboard specials range from grilled ribeye sandwich to shrimp gumbo.

Details: Breakfast, lunch and dinner daily. Credit cards. No bar.

Downtown Cafe
101 W. Church St., Weatherford
817-594-8717

Why go: Operating in a historic building on the pretty Parker County Courthouse Square, this old-school cafe does a lot of dishes impressively, whether old-school country cooking or freshened-up versions of restaurant classics. The owners love good food and do a lot toward bringing that passion to your plate.

In the know: The cafe closes at midafternoon Sundays through Wednesdays, so don't get caught short of supper!

Picks: Chicken-fried steak, chicken and dumplings, deep-fried Monte Cristo sandwich, avocado cheeseburger on a pretzel bun, blackberry cobbler, butterscotch pecan pancakes and veggie omelets keep crowds happy. Look for blackboard specials daily.

Details: Breakfast and lunch daily; dinner Thu-Sat. No bar.

Flatlanders Taco Company
109 Oakland St., Denton
940-387-4999, myflatlanders.com

Why go: Begun as a food truck, the Flatlanders popularity justified a brick-and-mortar location for enjoying the upscale renditions of street tacos. (The truck still operates, showing up at events around Denton, Dallas and Fort Worth environs.) The handsome interior of this aged building, which has housed a laundry, among other businesses, includes exposed brick walls, concrete floors, smooth wood tables and plentiful seating areas.

In the know: This is a hangout for more than the usual taco crowd. Look for vegan and vegetarian menu options, as well as gluten-free. There's also a solid coffeehouse vibe here, too; Addison Coffee Roasters products are poured.

Picks: Chicken tacos include chicken breast marinade in an orange-habanero blend, served with an avocado sauce. Tacos with steak marinated in chipotle and lime also include refried beans and pico de gallo. Still greater creativity shows up in crawfish-pineapple tacos and chipotle-lime tofu tacos. Tortas can be stuffed with anything from hatch chile pork to barbacoa.

Details: Lunch and dinner, Tue-Sun; brunch Sun. Credit cards. No bar.

Jake & Dorothy's
406 E. Washington St., Stephenville
254-965-5211

Why go: Since 1948, this old-fashioned cafe has been a popular stopping point for folks driving through Stephenville, and it's typically filled with locals, including students from Tarleton University.

In the know: The front room is smoky, so hold your breath till you make it to the non-smoking room. You'll pass the beautiful pie display cases en route. Be sure to check out the specials posted on handwritten signs on the walls.

Picks: The hamburger steak with grilled onions and brown gravy is outstanding, as are handmade burgers with waffle fries, chicken-fried steak and those amazing pies.

Details: Breakfast, lunch and dinner daily. Cash only. No bar.

Koffee Kup

300 W. Second St. (Texas 6 at U.S. 281), Hico
254-796-4839, koffeekupfamilyrestaurant.com

Why go: Popular since its opening in 1968, the KK is beloved for its mile-high pies, which many of us have been known to eat for breakfast. You can't help but take a photo of the sign hanging over the cash register that says, "Pie Fixes Everything." Because it does.

In the know: The Billy the Kid Museum is nearby, as is the sensational Wiseman House Chocolates. If you want to make an overnight stop here to do some shopping in Hico's cute historic downtown, book a room at the delightful Upstairs Inn (formerly Pecan Street Inn).

Picks: Chicken-fried steak and big yeast rolls are hard to pass up, and the giant onion rings are worth writing home about, too. But be sure to leave room for lemon, coconut, caramel or chocolate meringue pie.

Details: Breakfast, lunch and dinner daily. Cash only. No bar.

Loco Coyote
1795 County Road 1004, Glen Rose
254-897-2324

Why go: A good trek off the beaten path, this joint has served outrageously good barbecue and country cooking for many years. An ownership change in 2012 worked out just fine, as the pits are still turning out excellent 'cue.

In the know: If your order the Coyote Burger or a combination BBQ plate, understand that each is enough for three or four people. Expect lots of motorcycles in the parking lot and live music later in the evening, along with a long wait for tables at prime dining time.

Picks: That Coyote Burger comes topped with bacon, cheese, grilled onions and jalapeños and chili. The ribs are massive, to say nothing of very tasty. Chicken-fried steak is huge and very popular.

Details: Lunch Sat-Sun; dinner Thu-Sat. Full bar.

Malt Shop
2028 Fort Worth Highway, Weatherford
817-594-2524, maltshopweatherford.com

Why go: Since 1958, this little pink shack on a quiet stretch of U.S. 180 has been the place to go for good old-fashioned flat burgers and onion rings. It's an old drive-in that's now a walk-up spot with picnic tables outside; you order your food at the window and wait for your number to be called. Eat in your car if it's too cold, or at the well-worn tables under an awning in nicer weather.

In the know: Stop here for a bite before heading into Weatherford for the monthly flea market on weekends or the city's famous farmers' market, both near the Parker County Courthouse square.

Picks: Cheeseburger, BLT, onion rings and butterscotch shakes are classics.

Details: Lunch and dinner daily. No bar.

Mary's Cafe
119 Grant Ave., Strawn
254-672-5741

Why go: Since its opening in 1986, this jewel way out west of Fort Worth and south of Possum Kingdom Lake has been a mecca for people in search of exceptional chicken-fried steak. Travelers between the DFW area and Abilene plan their itineraries just to be sure they can make a detour for lunch or dinner in this area. You take exit 361 from Interstate 20 and drive north four miles on Texas 16, finding Mary's in a wide spot of the road on the right. You'll know it by the throng of trucks and cars parked outside.

In the know: If it's your birthday, call ahead and the kitchen will bake you a cake. During daytime hours, look a couple blocks north in the vintage downtown for An Ancient Art Handcrafted Soap Company, an aromatic little shop where wonderful soaps are made with olive oil.

Picks: Chicken-fried steak with hand-cut fries and salad is the way to go. The burger is excellent and enough for two very hungry people to share. Lemon meringue pie for dessert.

Details: Lunch and dinner daily. Beer and wine.

Ranchman's Cafe
110 W. Bailey St., Ponder
940-479-2221, ranchman.com

Why go: This old-fashioned country steakhouse has been a destination dining spot for folks all over the DFW area since 1948. Today's cafe owners say the spirit of Grace "Pete" Jackson, who opened the tiny cafe next to her family's grocery business, still fills the nooks and crannies of this creaky old joint. Countless farmers, ranchers, horse trainers, families and tourists have come through that banging screen door in front for a home-cooked meal and friendly service over the years.

In the know: If you want a baked potato with your steak, call ahead to reserve it. All steaks are cut to order, which explains the sawing noises you can hear from the kitchen.

Picks: Rib-eye is primo, but you can't lose with a T-bone or chicken-fried steak, either. Chicken and quail are good, too. The 24-ounce porterhouse is a fine choice for two.

Details: Lunch and dinner daily. BYOB.

Village Kitchen
934 S. Main St., Jacksboro
940-567-5902

Why go: This traditional coffee shop has brought in a good crowd since its opening in 1979. Folksy waitstaff make you feel at home, and who can resist a T-shirt that says, "Your momma's food might be better but she eats here when she's not cookin' "? Among the loyal clientele is Pulitzer-winning author Larry McMurtry, who's been known to bring visiting friends from nearby Archer City (his hometown and site of his Booked Up bookstore) just to eat the pies.

In the know: Fill up on grub here before visiting nearby Fort Richardson State Park and Historic Site and hiking the Lost Creek Reservoir State Trailway.

Picks: Chicken-fried steak, burgers and onion rings, Spanish omelets and chocolate pie are excellent.

Details: Breakfast and lunch daily; dinner Mon-Fri. No bar.

South Texas

Anita's Café
2102 N. McColl Rd, Edinburg
956-318-0730

Why go: The tagline, "the real sabor of Old Mexico," says it all. This friendly, bustling family operation offers the best of the Rio Grande Valley and makes everything from scratch. The signature South Texas appetizer platter called botanas is spot-on, with all the goodies for one or for many to share. There's a full breakfast menu, too, as well as lunch specials ranging from chicken enchiladas to carne guisada. Burgers are among big hits, as well.

In the know: The tortilla lady busily making tortillas by hand tells you this is as authentic as you can hope to find.

Picks: Locals love the $9.99 buffet, which features a rotating selection of entrees, along with fresh salads and a dessert selection. Favorites include brisket and barbecued chicken, as well as arroz con pollo, mole enchiladas and pork chops in salsa. The restaurant's Facebook page updates the daily offerings.

Details: Breakfast and lunch daily. Credit cards. No bar.

Caro's Restaurant
607 W. Second St., Rio Grande City
956-487-2255

Why go: A mainstay in the Rio Grande Valley since the 1930s, Caro's was opened at a motel by a widow with six small children. It's moved since then, but the Tex-Mex food is still hearty and the service, overseen by members of the original family, is friendly.

In the know: The nearby La Borde House, an 1899 home converted a hotel, is a big attraction for those seeking haunted houses. Trolley tours around town take place twice daily on weekdays.

Picks: The signature puffy tacos are worth the trip alone, but there are good enchiladas and arroz con pollo, too.

Details: Lunch and dinner daily. Full bar.

The Centennial Club
1410 Austin Ave., McAllen
956-627-6257, thecentennialclub.com

Why go: Bearing every earmark of a speakeasy, this bistro was formerly called White Kitchen Café. Occupying one of McAllen's historic downtown buildings, it's an experience unto itself in the Rio Grande Valley.

In the know: Fancier than any cafes around, there's nevertheless a homegrown quality about the place. Regional influences are strong in dishes found in each of the menu's six distinctive sections.

Picks: Roasted corn, cut from the cob, is tossed in a housemade spicy aioli and topped with fried cilantro. Quail breast is stuffed with jalapeno, wrapped in smoky bacon and doused with a chimmichuri sauce.

Details: Dinner, Tue-Sat. Credit cards. Full bar.

Charlie's Corona
3902 San Bernardo Ave., Laredo
956-725-8227

Why go: Texas' border towns may be packed with Mexican restaurants, but Charlie's scores big with both locals and tourists for food and atmosphere.

In the know: A live-music program frequently features Tejano bands. If you're perusing the Facebook page, it helps to read Spanish.

Picks: Check out daily specials on the board, from T-bone steak to tilapia to seafood enchiladas. Menu favorites include buffalo chicken strips and chicken-fried steak.

Details: Lunch daily; dinner Tue-Sat. Full bar.

Danny's Mexican Restaurant
2408 W. Griffin Parkway, Mission
956-580-3330

Why go: Certainly, there's no shortage of places to find home-style Mexican food in the Valley, as it's pretty much on every corner. But Danny's, open since 1986, is known through the RGV for food that's a cut above much of the rest. Surprisingly homey and friendly for a place that can seat more than 100, it's even open on major holidays. Its popularity has led to the opening of two other Danny's in Mission.

In the know: Plan a trip to Danny's before or after visiting the fantastic World Birding Center at Bentsen-Rio Grande State Park. It's on your way, coming or going. Look also downtown for murals celebrating hometown son Tom Landry, the legendary Dallas Cowboys coach.

Picks: Danny's old-school combo platters are famous in the Valley; the cheese enchiladas are as classic Tex-Mex as it gets. The breakfast menu encompasses all the typical options, both Tex-Mex and American, as well as some interesting outliers like eggs and barbacoa or scrambled eggs with machaca (dried beef).

Details: Breakfast, lunch and dinner daily. No bar.

Las Vegas Restaurant
1101 West Harrison Ave., Harlingen
956-423-6749

Why go: Once you're a regular, the waitresses call you by name and make you feel completely at home. That's why there's often a line out the door for a table at breakfast at this Tex-Mex classic.

In the know: Harlingen is often a jumping-off place en route to South Padre Island; you can fly into the Valley International Airport or make a pit stop here on driving trips to the beach.

Picks: Chorizo and eggs with potatoes at breakfast; enchiladas with rice and beans or carne guisada and picadillo tacos at lunch and dinner — all are budget-priced. Diners wash it all down with the huge glasses of sweet tea.

Details: Breakfast, lunch and dinner Mon-Sat. No bar.

Longhorn Cattle Company
3055 W. U.S. 83, San Benito
956-399-4400, longhorncattlecompany.com

Why go: Good barbecue in the Rio Grande Valley isn't abundant, so this place is a find. It's a rambling place with friendly and quick service.

In the know: Everyone touts the barbecue, but the mesquite-grilled rib-eye is a good choice, too. As you fill up, you can watch the cattle and horses grazing out the window in an adjacent pasture.

Picks: Combo plates offer two or three meats; tables of four or more can order family-style and get an all-you-can eat parade of all the smoked meats — brisket, Polish sausage, chicken, turkey breast and pork ribs. All come with potato salad, coleslaw, pickles, onions, bead and the very popular pinto bean soup.

Details: Lunch and dinner Tue-Sun. Beer and wine.

Rex Cafe & Bakery
321 S. 17th St., McAllen
956-686-9074

Why go: Rogelio Guerrero opened his doors after returning from war in 1947, and Rex has remained a family business ever since. The vintage photography inside is worth perusing.

In the know: Quite close by is the Casa de Palmas Renaissance Hotel, a beautiful historic property with a gorgeous tiled courtyard, Spanish-villa architecture and a pleasant bar.

Picks: Pan dulce, the Mexican pastries so beloved by regulars, are perfect with morning coffee or afternoon tea. Huevos rancheros and chilaquiles remain the most popular breakfast dishes, as they have for generations.

Details: Breakfast, lunch and dinner daily. No bar.

Toddle Inn
1740 Central Blvd., Brownsville
956-542-8838

Why go: This early-'60s relic has grown from a tiny place with just four tables to one accommodating up to 100 people. Nevertheless, it still feels like a comfortable little cafe.

In the know: The Gladys Porter Zoo in Brownsville remains a primary attraction in the Rio Grande Valley, but Brownsville's greatest asset is its proximity to South Padre Island.

Picks: Tamales, beef or chicken caldo (soup), bistec ranchero, T-bone steak and seafood platters all have their fans. The breakfast tacos, big burritos and various egg plates are popular, too.

Details: Open for breakfast and lunch daily. No bar.

Panhandle, Plains & Far West Texas

Allen's Family Style Meals
1301 E. Broadway St., Sweetwater
325-235-2060

Why go: Opened in 1952 as Mrs. Allen's, this was a boarding-house-style dining room in a family home where Mrs. Lizzie Allen served dinner, the familiar name for lunch in these parts. The food is still plentiful today, to say the least, and it's country cooking, so don't expect anything fancy.

In the know: At lunchtime, food is served family-style.

Picks: Fried chicken is the dish Allen's is famous for, but other goodies include meatloaf, roast beef and a wide variety of sides, from mashed potatoes and squash to green beans and potato salad. Banana pudding and hot rolls are big favorites, too.

Details: Lunch Tue-Sun. No bar.

Big Boy's Bar-B-Que
2117 Lamar St., Sweetwater
325-235-2700

Why go: Big Boy's sits in a desolate area but is well worth finding. Another of *Texas Monthly*'s top-50 'cue joints, this one grabs attention for pitmaster Gaylan Marth's mesquite-smoked goods.

In the know: Sweetwater sits right on Interstate 20, about 225 miles west of Dallas and 400 miles east of El Paso. Besides Allen's (see above), there's not much else to eat between here and Lubbock, 122 miles north of Sweetwater, so you should plan on lunch or early dinner right here.

Picks: Well-rubbed beef brisket is worth the trip, as are pork ribs, covered in a caramelized glaze and offered in both a traditional style and a country style, cut from the pork butt (which is actually the shoulder of the pig, by the way). Key lime pie is a good finish.

Details: Lunch and dinner Wed-Sat; closed Sun-Tue. No bar.

Coney Island Cafe
114 W. Foster St., Pampa
806-669-9137

Why go: A small-town gathering spot since 1933, this shotgun space in a rather lonely downtown is often filled with teenagers, local police and tables of coffee-klatschers. They come in for chili dogs and linger at the retro counter and booths for the dozen or so choices in homemade pies. Opened by Greek immigrants, as was the case with many such coffee shops in Depression-era Texas, Coney Island is one of a dying breed.

In the know: Specials include beef-vegetable stew, which can be soothing when a blue norther is blowing through the Panhandle in this oil town northeast of Amarillo.

Picks: Whatever you do, don't pass up the pie. In fact, get two pieces. Buttermilk, cherry cream, coconut, chocolate and peanut butter are all fine choices.

Details: Lunch and early dinner Mon-Sat; closed Sun. No bar.

El Tejavan
3420 Interstate 40 West, Amarillo
806-354-2444, eltejavan.com

Why go: Begun as a convenience store dining stop, this is now a destination spot in the Panhandle. Named el tejavan for the front porch the owners stuck on their original taco shop, it's popular morning, noon and night.

In the know: New Mexico's influence pops up on the menu, with green and red chile sauces and flat enchilada stacks. But Texas influences come through loud and clear with fajitas selections as well. Huevos divorciados is a favorite from old Mexico, served at breakfast.

Picks: Appetizers include a jack cheese melted with jalapenos, onion and tomato, mingling with chopped pork or beef, perfect for sweeping into hot tortillas; and a cup of whole bean soup, cooked with bacon and pork skin. The favorite enchilada dish is the stacked version, a layering of corn tortillas with cheese and marinated beef, with two over-easy eggs atop.

Details: Breakfast and lunch daily; dinner, Mon-Sat. Credit cards. Full bar.

Fort Griffin General Merchandise Restaurant and Beehive Saloon

517 U.S. 180 West, Albany
325-675-0600, beehivesaloon.com

Why go: Opened in 1981 by the Esfandiary brothers when they were based at Dyess Air Force Base near Abilene, this jewel of a steakhouse has won a fan base stretching all the way to Dallas and across West Texas (there's a second location in Abilene). The steaks can be as good as those found in big cities, and the wine list is impressive, too. It's all housed in a cluster of buildings with Old West wooden false fronts; everybody just refers to the complex as "the Beehive."

In the know: Drinking at the bar, next door to the fancier dining rooms, requires the purchase of a private membership for a small fee, as Shackelford County is dry. Crowds are huge during Fandangle, the three-quarter-century-old outdoor pageant held in late June in Albany. And folks come to Albany from all over, year-round, to visit the impressive Old Jail Art Center, where you can view works by Modigliani, Klee and Renoir; a sizable Asian art collection; and contemporary exhibits from notable Texas artists. Plenty of folks come to hunt, too, in Shackelford County, where Texas ranching traditions (and oil) run deep.

Picks: Prime rib, rib-eye steak, rack of lamb and grilled zucchini all win raves.

Details: Lunch and dinner Tue-Sat; closed Sun-Mon. Full bar.

Golden Light Cafe
2908 S.W. Sixth Ave., Amarillo
806-374-9237, goldenlightcafe.com

Why go: A hamburger joint and bar on old Route 66, this 1946 landmark is a lovably creaky place with neon beer signs and cooking that would never be approved by the American Heart Association. The regulars mosey in and plan to sit a spell, waiting on handmade burgers and other platters of food, which go well with cold longneck beer. Grab a booth and be ready to travel back in time.

In the know: There's live music playing several nights a week in the cantina attached. Nearby, find lots of antiques shops lining the old avenue, which is the historic Route 66, also known as the Mother Road.

Picks: Flagstaff Pie is known as Frito Pie to the rest of us. We also like the green-chile burger wrapped in a big flour tortilla.

Details: Lunch and dinner Mon-Sat; closed Sun. Beer and wine.

Lee's Café
1101 Main St., Lubbock
806-368-8537, leescafelubbock.com

Why go: Great soul food in the Panhandle and South Plains is a true find, especially when paired with good sandwiches and burgers. The setting is pure old-school Texana, with murals of Buddy Holly and other yesteryear idols on the walls.

In the know: The family-owned operation isn't old but has a wonderful vintage feel to it. Service is friendly and the food is handmade.

Picks: The crunchy fried chicken is the way to go, but the chicken fried steak topped with peppery cream gravy makes the decision tough. Then there are fried or grilled pork chops, smothered hamburger steak and fried catfish just to complicate things. Meals come with two sides (mashed potatoes, green beans, collard greens, cabbage and yams, among others) and cornbread muffins. There's a fine barbecued link sandwich, too, along with chicken and waffles. Oh, and daily specials range from meat loaf to smothered ribs.

Details: Lunch and early dinner, Mon-Fri. Credit cards. No bar.

Old Sutphen's
303 N. Cedar St., Borger
806-273-6442

Why go: Here's what happens when a barbecue joint becomes a bar and grill, too. You get the best of all worlds, with small-town friendliness to spare.

In the know: Aiming to please all appetites, this restaurant rounds out selections with salads (chicken fajita, chicken Caesar), tortilla soup and fruit salad with a side of cottage cheese for those skipping the barbecue indulgence.

Picks: A sampler platter combines ribs, brisket, sausage and pork for a pound total. Beef nachos will fill you up, as well. Just don't skip the killer onion rings.

Details: Lunch and dinner daily. Credit cards. Full bar.

Perini Ranch Steak House
3002 FM 89, Buffalo Gap
325-572-3339, periniranch.com

Why go: After a decade of catering ranch events chuckwagon-style, lifelong ranchman Tom Perini decided to convert one of his old ranch buildings into a steakhouse in 1983— and he's never looked back. A rustic, unpretentious place that serves exceptionally good food, Perini Ranch has become famous on a national scale. Tom and wife Lisa Perini have served dinner to a number of presidents, and their restaurant has received one of the most coveted awards from New York's James Beard Foundation, which named Perini Ranch one of America's Classics in 2014.

In the know: The expansive Buffalo Gap compound includes a renovated farmhouse and nearby "camp house" for lodging. Be sure to pick up a copy of Perini's cookbook, *Texas Cowboy Cooking*, with a foreword written by Tom's friend, actor Robert Duvall. Perini also sells his heavenly mesquite-smoked peppered whole beef tenderloin online. If you're into great wine and celebrity chefs, buy a ticket for the Buffalo Gap Wine & Food Summit, held at the end of April at Perini Ranch Steakhouse.

Picks: The rib-eye steak and mesquite-smoked prime rib are Perini specialties. We also like the green-chile hominy, as well as the fried chicken served at Sunday lunch.

Details: Lunch Fri-Sun; dinner Tue-Sun. Full bar.

Pody's BBQ
1330 S. Cedar St., Pecos
432-448-4635

Why go: *Texas Monthly* deemed this one of the top 50 barbecue joints in the state in 2013, so you know it's worth finding. Using mesquite, cherry, pecan and oak wood to smoke the meats, owner Pody Campos, who's also the county's chief deputy, also has a fondness for very hot chiles in his sauce.

In the know: Pecos, which bills itself as the home of the world's first rodeo, is the home of a fine little historical museum, the West of the Pecos Museum. It's also renowned for growing some of the best cantaloupes in Texas.

Picks: Brisket is the choice of experts here. Be sure to order a large iced tea.

Details: Lunch Tue-Sat; closed Sun-Mon. No bar.

Tyler's Barbeque
2014 Paramount Blvd., Amarillo
806-331-2271, tylersbarbeque.com

Why go: Included in *Texas Monthly*'s top-50 report in 2013, this barbecue joint has won legions of fans in a relatively short time. Like most good barbecue places, it's not fancy, but the food is outstanding.

In the know: Don't go late in the day, expecting ribs to last until closing. Frequently, these sell out. And the food's best when it's freshest from the pit.

Picks: Beef brisket with a beautiful crust is excellent, as are pork ribs, smoked over mesquite wood. The house sauce is a peppery version with a little sweetness. Jalapeño-cheddar sausage earns high marks, as does the mac-and-cheese.

Details: Lunch and dinner Tue-Sat; closed Sun-Mon. No bar.

Youngblood's Stockyard Cafe
620 S.W. 16th Ave., Amarillo
806-342-9411, stockyardscafeamarillo.com

Why go: Relocated to downtown from its longtime site in the Amarillo stockyards, this cafe brings together Texas food sensibilities with fine cooking. Owner Tim Youngblood is a graduate of the Culinary Institute of America in New York and cooked at the Plaza Hotel's Oak Room in NYC before returning to his roots in the Panhandle.

In the know: Take lots of hungry folks with you, as the plates here are overwhelmingly generous. Breakfast is served all day (with the exception of pancakes and burritos).

Picks: Green chile-cheese omelet is our favorite in the morning; at lunch or dinner, we like the BLT with avocado, rib-eye steak, chicken-fried steak and Cajun catfish.

Details: Breakfast and lunch daily. No bar.